PORTRAIT OF GOD

Jack Mooring

PORTRAIT OF GOD

*Rediscovering the Attributes of God
through the Stories of His People*

DAVID **C** COOK®

transforming lives together

PORTRAIT OF GOD
Published by David C Cook
4050 Lee Vance Drive
Colorado Springs, CO 80918 U.S.A.

Integrity Music Limited, a Division of David C Cook
Brighton, East Sussex BN1 2RE, England

DAVID C COOK® and related marks are registered
trademarks of David C Cook.

The website addresses recommended throughout this book are offered as a
resource to you. These websites are not intended in any way to be or imply an
endorsement on the part of David C Cook, nor do we vouch for their content.

Unless otherwise noted, all Scripture quotations are taken from the ESV® Bible
(The Holy Bible, English Standard Version®), copyright © 2001 by Crossway, a
publishing ministry of Good News Publishers. Used by permission. All rights
reserved; KJV are taken from the King James Version of the Bible. (Public
Domain.); NKJV are taken from the New King James Version®. Copyright
© 1982 by Thomas Nelson. Used by permission. All rights reserved.

The author has added italics to Scripture quotations for emphasis.

Library of Congress Control Number: 2023945301
ISBN 978-0-8307-8603-9
eISBN 978-0-8307-8628-2

© 2024 Jack Mooring
Published in association with the literary agency WTA
Media, LLC, in Franklin, Tennessee.

The Team: Michael Covington, Jeff Gerke, Gina Pottenger,
Leigh Davidson, James Hershberger, Susan Murdock
Cover Design: Brian Mellema

Printed in the United States of America
First Edition 2024

1 2 3 4 5 6 7 8 9 10

050624

*To my wife, whose unwavering support
and love made this book possible.*

CONTENTS

ACKNOWLEDGMENTS

I owe a great debt of gratitude to my wife and children, who have supported me throughout the long process of writing this book. Thank you to my church, Celebration of Life: Nashville, and our mother church, COL Baytown, who have been so kind and encouraging as I have gotten this project over the finish line.

Thank you to Dr. George Grant, who has been a great influence on my life and who was the first to introduce me to Thomas Chalmers. Thank you to Anne Severance, my wonderful grandmother-in-law who helped edit the manuscript in its early stages, and to my developmental editor, Jeff Gerke, whose input was invaluable.

Thank you to Dave Schroeder and Michael Covington, who have helped bring this book to the wider public.

I would like to thank my mom, dad, brother, and sister as well as my brother-in-law and sister-in-law, who were always there to cheer me on whenever I sent them an excerpt.

Finally, thank You to the one true faithful God whose patience is immeasurable. He believes in our dreams, and His grace brings them to life.

FOREWORD

How do we hold on to unchangeable truth when everything seems to be changing so fast?

Perhaps we should look into the nature and attributes of God, who never changes, and to the example of those in the past who have clung to Him during their own struggles with an ever-shifting world.

Their stories bring hope and encouragement to our own—since each of our lives is a story in progress! And our constant, steady, and loving God is the same One who walked them through their lives and is walking us through ours.

Portrait of God is a beautiful, compelling mix of storytelling and theology, biography, and Bible. The stories of the men and women of God that you will read in these pages will draw you into their cultures and even their emotions.

Jack does a masterful job of letting us know that these forefathers and mothers were real, breathing, laughing, and crying people who needed God's grace and provision. And the qualities abundant in God's nature (love, joy, compassion, faithfulness) are abundantly available to us and perfectly suited to the challenges of our own culture.

Yes, Jack Mooring is our son-in-law, and yes, we can report from personal experience that he is a kind and loving father, friend, and pastor (and family comedian on many occasions!). But we champion this book for a reason removed from any of those associations: We need it! We need to hear (and rehear) the powerful stories of godly people who went before us. We need these deep insights into the Word of God that will help inform and equip us to stay the course and finish well, by the grace of a God who never changes.

We wonder if you just might need it too?

Grateful to be His,

Michael W. and Debbie Smith

INTRODUCTION

A few years ago, I set out on a journey to write my first book. As I began writing, an idea quickly struck me. The idea I couldn't get away from was God Himself. The more I thought and wrote about God, the more my roller coaster of life experiences with Him confronted me (as did the experiences of my friends).

There have been times in my life when I felt so close to Him and was filled with such a clear sense of who He was. Other times, it seemed like my mind was muddled and He was far away. But through it all, I've learned that the Christian life is less about learning and more about remembering.

I grew up in a rich tradition of truth, but life's lies have often buried those true ideas about God. So I wrote this book to remind myself and the rest of us forgetful people that this God we love is really who He says He is. This book is an attempt to rediscover our wonder about who He is. To "paint God" and "re-image" Him in our minds and hearts.

How do we do this? Each chapter explores an attribute of God's character. Of course, there are far more aspects of God than we could ever cover in this book, but I chose some that I feel are necessary to understand if we want the life that is possible in Christ.

Not too long into the writing process, I began to feel that the chapters needed one more element. I wanted to show you what these ideas look like in real life and not just tell you about the concepts. So, for each attribute of God, I chose a person in church history who actually experienced that part of God's nature. (All except for the first chapter, which uses a fictional parable to start us off.) The goal is that, as we hear the stories of these people, we can get a glimpse of God through their eyes.

So, what attributes of God do we cover in the book?

We start with a chapter on God's love, which is the great motivator of all His actions. Love isn't something outside Him but originates in Him, and all His other attributes cannot be understood apart from this.

> The Christian life is less about learning
> and more about remembering.

Next, we explore God's joy. We live in a world of anxious people who fear the future. So much of modern psychology is about finding happiness, and people desperately and feverishly search for it. In this chapter, we find that joy comes from God—the author of color and laughter! His joy is not a superficial or shallow happiness; rather, it is a deep river that remains constant, even through real pain and suffering. We hear the story of C. S. Lewis, who experienced this joy not in a life free from hardship but amid loss and frustration. And we find that the joy God offers is much richer than anything the world can give us.

After this, we consider God's holiness. I chose to highlight this attribute because it is not only central to who God is, but it is a deeply misunderstood word in our culture. In this chapter, we hear the story of Augustine of Hippo, who experienced God's holiness not just as a set of rules to follow but as a deep source of life and peace. His journey to holiness didn't begin behind the walls of a monastery but amid the fast-paced sensuality of city life.

And then, we read about God's compassion for the hurting in the lives of William and Catherine Booth, founders of the Salvation Army, for whom God's compassion wasn't merely a quaint concept but a practical power for serving the poor.

In a book about God's attributes, we cannot avoid the subject of miracles. The life of Kathryn Kuhlman reminds us that God is truly all powerful. He is the God who works signs and wonders. We discuss this often-misunderstood subject and what it means for us today.

We see God's transforming grace in Thomas Chalmers's encounter with the gospel, and we discover God's faithfulness from the story of Fanny Crosby. From her, we discover that even in great personal suffering, His goodness doesn't change or leave us.

Finally, we find God's truth in the life of one of the church's greatest theologians, the Egyptian church father Athanasius.

I mentioned that I wrote this book for us forgetful believers, but I also wrote with another group in mind. I thought of those who have never met this God or who have been told all sorts of lies and distortions about Him. I hope these glimpses into God and those who knew Him will serve as an open door into faith for anyone seeking answers.

Finally, in an age of glittering distractions and dizzying change, we need an anchor to hold on to. This anchor is God Himself.

Paul encourages us to consider the "breadth and length and height and depth, and to know the love of Christ that surpasses knowledge" that we "may be filled with all the fullness of God" (Eph. 3:18–19).

The Christian life is a continual rhythm of remembering. We must return to the One who made us. Because in gazing upon Him, we will not only find our purpose but will actually fulfill our purpose, because we were made to know Him.

Chapter 1

"THE PAINTER"— GOD OF LOVE

If you live in the Western world, chances are you've heard the phrase "God loves you." If you grew up in the church like I did, you've heard it thousands of times.

Why do we have such a hard time believing it when many of us know the story by heart? What is this tendency in us to resist the goodness of God? This book explores those questions and more.

But ultimately this book is about understanding who God really is. What is He like? What can we discover about His character through some of the people who knew Him, walked with Him, were changed by Him? By learning their stories, we will get to know God a little more—and as we gaze upon Him, we will find our purpose.

Let's start with the core of His identity. The deep motivation of our great painter God: love. We must paint a portrait of the painter.

Getting Her Back (A Parable)

She was alone again. The museum was closed, and the last tourists had left hours ago. The great halls were now dark as thick clouds crept high over the skylights. Not even the moon was allowed in tonight.

She hated these long, quiet hours that left her alone with her thoughts, and she jealously longed for sleep. At least the humans could escape the real world for a few hours. Not her. She hung there in the stillness waiting for the sun to rise and the crowds to return.

Then she heard footsteps. The hushed voices came low and deliberate as their sound drew closer. One voice was immediately recognizable. Henri Lorain had been curator for only a year but had grown up in these halls. She had always been fond of him. He was not alone, though, and his guest with gray hair seemed to be walking twice as fast. She froze her lips into that vague expression of amusement just in time for them to turn the corner. They came right toward her, stopping no more than two feet away.

They were silent for a moment, awkward as though not sure how to get to the point.

"You said you had new information on her provenance," Henri said, breaking the silence.

"Yes, yes," came the reply in a thick Italian accent. The man with gray hair had not dropped his gaze from her eyes since they had approached. He seemed transfixed.

Lorenzo looked intently at her, a painting he had seen a thousand times, but she somehow looked new tonight, with a beauty he had not seen in her before. "Well," he said, continuing to look into her eyes, "I wanted you to be the first to hear it. As you well know, not long after the painting was finished, she was stolen by thieves in Florence and sold to an unknown buyer."

Henri nodded. "Yes, the artist lost her, and she was found by the museum in the early nineteenth century."

Lorenzo turned to Henri and spoke in a whisper as if not to be overheard. "Everything we've been told is a lie. Yes, the painting was lost. The artist spent his whole life trying to find it. It became an obsession for him. I've recently found proof.

Documents, letters. It's taken me quite some time to confirm their authenticity. But they are real."

"What do they say?" Henri asked nervously.

"Not long after the artist's eightieth birthday, he heard of a wealthy aristocrat in southern France who had amassed a great art collection, including works from the Italian greats. The artist had already scoured most of Europe looking for his beloved painting, so when he heard about this collector, he knew he must go there immediately. The painter made the long journey over the French Pyrenees and finally arrived after weeks of travel. When he arrived at the estate, he was shown every piece of art in the halls and grand ballrooms, but she was nowhere to be found."

As Henri listened to Lorenzo's excited whispers, the darkened museum seemed to fade, and it was as if he were watching the scene play out before his eyes. He felt he himself were the artist standing with the French lord, having just seen the last of the man's great collection.

"Is there anything else?" the artist asked in a tired voice.

"Oui," the lord said. "Also in our cellar we have a few works."

"Please take me there!" he exclaimed, his heart beating desperately. They wound down the damp stone stairs into what looked more like a dungeon than a cellar. The claws of unseen rodents skittered on the wet, black floor.

There she was. Leaning against a stone wall, half obscured by other paintings, only her hair visible. The artist carefully removed the other paintings to reveal her face, and he began to weep. Marred by years of neglect and dirt, she smiled at him as beautifully as he had remembered her.

Losing all sense of decorum, he turned sharply to the lord. "I must have her back! How much?"

Sensing his desperation, the shrewd aristocrat gave a figure that was cruelly extravagant.

To pay such a fee would cost the painter everything. He would have to sell his life's work, his home, and every one of his belongings to raise the amount. Without hesitation, he simply said, "Yes."

Henri came back to the present as Lorenzo brought his story to a close.

"When the painter died years later, he was found in a small home on the outskirts of Florence. There was a bed, a table with two chairs, and some books. Hanging on the wall was the breathtaking portrait of her face. He left it in his will to the people of Italy with these words: 'I gave everything I had to paint her. And I gave everything I had to get her back. I give her to you now, so the world may enjoy her beauty as much as I have.'"

The Standard

We hold ourselves to a standard, and we know we are not reaching it. It's like a ceiling we can't touch or a status we will never attain. The standard of being good, gifted, kind, pure, honest, productive, excellent, beautiful, strong. We all have our list. And even on the days when we are "good," we are bullied by what could have been better. Even the best days end, and we wake to hear the crack of the gun starting another race to God knows where.

They can call us "beautiful" all they want, but we know the *real* us. They can say we are gifted, but they don't see our secret and shameful knowledge of wasted opportunities. Even at our best, we are never quite enough for our own exacting standards.

Where did these standards come from anyway? Oh, yeah! God! *He* is good, gifted, kind, pure, honest, productive, excellent, beautiful, and strong. How do we even know what these things are except that they are from Him first? Every standard we set sees its fulfillment in Him. He does not just meet every standard; He is the standard.

We relentlessly hustle to measure up to God. And it is, of course, absurd.

It is like the *Mona Lisa* hating herself because she is not da Vinci! Even though millions of people come to adore her, it is not enough. She wants legs and lungs and a beating heart. But this, of course, is not possible because she is a painting and can never be the painter. She is a created thing, and he is the creator.

One of the fundamental problems with our world is that, even though we are not God, we desperately try, in some form or another, to make ourselves gods. All sorts of disappointment and suffering follow.

There is another problem too. And it is just as damaging.

The Painter Loves His Work

If the first problem is about us not being God, the second is about us not pleasing God. What if the *Mona Lisa* were a living being, and what if she came to grips with the fact that she was just a painting and she would never be the painter? Yay! Freedom! She's free to just *be*.

But imagine that one day someone in the line of people looking at her said, "I can't believe this painting is so popular. Did you know da Vinci never even really liked it?"

Someone with bad information or ill intent spoke this lie, of course. But that never really matters, does it? What matters was that she heard it. This person simply stated what the *Mona Lisa* had suspected all along: She wasn't who everyone thought she was. She was a fraud who would be found out. That although the whole world loved her, she didn't have the love of the one who had created her.

Often, religious culture tells us this lie about God. We hear somewhere along the way that the painter really doesn't like the painting. "This painter has exacting standards! He is a genius, after all, so it takes something *truly* special to please Him." The second problem goes something like this: "Yeah, sure ... God created me, but He doesn't like me. I am a disappointment. He has a standard for me that I am not meeting, and He is not happy about it. I am not enough for Him."

The whole story arc of Scripture works to dispel this lie. God the Father—God the creator, God the painter—is shouting to us through His Word, through creation, through the gospel, through Jesus, saying, "You do not embarrass Me! I didn't create you to discard you! I created you to celebrate you! And my deepest desire is for you to be close to Me!"

What Is He Like?

God's love is an overwhelming topic. And rightly so, since God Himself is overwhelming. He has limitless knowledge. Limitless power. There is no place in which He does not exist and no time He is not currently experiencing. In other words, God knows everything, He can do anything, and He exists everywhere and at all times.

I don't know about you, but that makes me a bit nervous. I was a teenager when the movie *I Know What You Did Last Summer* came out. I always found that to be an eerie title. Well, God does literally know what you did last summer. Because He was there. Not only was He there, but He perceived it all perfectly, including our sins, with His piercing intellect. He is powerful enough to vaporize us for it, and He would have to answer to no one if He did. His raw power is truly overwhelming! But is that all there is to the story? A terrifying God? Is He just a cosmic intelligence? An all-seeing eye?

His omniscience, omnipotence, and omnipresence are interesting (if not frightening) facts about Him. But they are still just cold facts. So the real question remains, "What is He *like*?"

Imagine you asked me to describe my father to you. I respond in a monotone: "He is six feet tall. Two hundred and twenty-four pounds. Sixty-one years old with blue eyes." This may be accurate, but it tells you nothing about who he really is. What are his quirks, tendencies, interests, and habits? How did he react when I forgot to take the trash out? Or when I scored a goal in the soccer game?

Many of the poor descriptions of God haven't been wrong—they've just been incomplete. Or they have started with the technical descriptors and then made bad assumptions about His nature based on those. Much like trying to figure out the deepest workings of someone's heart by looking at the clothes she wears or the color of her skin.

Just because God is powerful doesn't mean He's abusive. Just because God is everywhere doesn't mean He's invasive. And just because He knows everything doesn't mean He's oppressive. In fact, central to His character is another element. It radiates from the core of His being, animating and motivating His actions. He uses all His knowledge, power, and presence so we can experience it. God's core motivator is His love.

He Thought of You

God is "uncreated," which means He never had a beginning. Before we existed as objects of love, He existed as the source from which love flows. Blazing alone, fully sufficient, and in need of nothing.

This makes Ephesians 1 even more stunning. Not just that God loved us, but that He even thought to make us! His inexplicable decision amazes me still.

God was already completely fulfilled within Himself. Father, Son, and Holy Spirit perfectly one. C. S. Lewis refers to the trinity as "a kind of dance."[1] That party didn't need any more guests!

Have you ever tried to get a gift for the person who "has everything"? You try to find something the person would want but doesn't already have. God gave Himself the gift of humanity. And when someone needs nothing, the only things he keeps are the things he wants. God needed nothing yet wanted you!

The most significant moment in human history was when the all-sufficient One decided there should *be* a human history. He purposed in His heart to invent objects on which to shower His goodness.

The Hairs on Your Head

> Are not two sparrows sold for a copper coin? And not one of them falls to the ground apart from your Father's will. But the very hairs of your head are all numbered. Do not fear therefore; you are of more value than many sparrows. (Matt. 10:29–31 NKJV)

This is such an interesting Bible passage. Earlier in the chapter, Jesus prepared His disciples for inevitable persecution. He says, "They will deliver you over to courts and flog you in their synagogues" (v. 17), and "you will be hated by all for my name's sake" (v. 22a). He goes so far as to say, "Brother will deliver brother over to death, and the father his child, and children will rise against parents and have them put to death" (v. 21). I can imagine the disciples standing wide-eyed at the end of such an encouraging sermon.

Fear, at its core, is disbelief in God's love.

Then Jesus says, "So have no fear of them, for nothing is covered that will not be revealed" (v. 26), and He goes on to talk about sparrows in the air and hairs on our head.

It was such a strange way to comfort His disciples. He could have said, "Don't worry. I'm really strong and I'll fight the people persecuting you!" Instead, He encouraged them with something greater than that: He reminded them about His thoughts for them. He is the God who cares about sparrows. He is the God who counts hair. Jesus tells the disciples that they are more valuable than "many sparrows" (v. 31).

Why is this comforting? Jesus is saying to them, "Of course, I'm powerful. Of course, I will bring justice in the end. But the most important thing for you to know is that I love you. You are valuable to Me. Those are the thoughts I'm thinking toward you! And when you experience persecution, remind yourself that the Father knows everything you are going through. He knows what He is doing. And you are of infinite worth to Him."

Fear Not

"Fear not, for I am with you" (Isa. 41:10).

Those seven words are some of the most comforting God has ever spoken to us. He is with you. It is such a beautifully simple statement. So emphatic. So clear. There is no misunderstanding what He is saying here. "Fear not, for I am with you." This is not only a loving promise from a good Father, but it's a nonnegotiable command from almighty God.

Fear not. A command to cease our worrying. To put an end to our striving. To just rest in the fact that His love surrounds us. For fear, at its core, is disbelief in God's love. Fear denies the promise that He is with us.

Do we really understand the seriousness of God's command for us to fear not? How much He cares about us? Many of us who grew up in church have a Sunday-school familiarity with God's love and power. We sing "Jesus loves me, this I know" and "Our God is so *big*, so strong, and so *mighty*!" But the deep-seated beliefs of our hearts forget His power ... forget His love. If only we would remember that He employs His power, His fierce nature, and His boundless energy all in pursuit of us.

It is the height of hubris to reject His pursuit. And it is the strategy of hell to make you forget He is pursuing you.

If we could only get a glimpse. If we could only understand that we are not a side project for God. That He is not a disinterested life force but has poured Himself out and made a way for us to know Him and be known by Him. In a society obsessed with being liked, we've forgotten that we have something better: love. Love from the only one who matters. From the only one capable of loving without error.

Fear not, for He is with you. Smile and rest in that truth.

He Knows Our Frame

One thing that fuels our distrust of God's love is our fear of rejection, our "not-enoughness." This feeling of being defective. A failure. That everyone else in the world has it together except you. If it weren't so destructive an idea, it would almost be comical. Picture billions of people walking around thinking they are the *only ones* who fail. It is silly. But it's a remarkably effective strategy of the enemy.

"He knows our frame," the psalmist penned (Ps. 103:14a). Our frame. I have a small frame. I'm about five foot seven ... when I wear the right shoes. And in my weaker moments, I've dreamed of being six foot three. Well, here's the problem: God *designed* me this way. God isn't wishing I were taller because He designed me to be five seven. He knows my frame.

In the same way, He knows the deep, hidden things we wrestle with or don't like about ourselves. He knows how He designed us, and He knows how the enemy distorts and manipulates the good in us.

God did not create any evil things—only good things that evil corrupts or distorts. Food, sex, art, literature, government, the church. All these things are good. God came up with all of them! But it is the distortion and idolization of these things, not the things themselves, that result in all kinds of evil.

It is the same way with you. God designed you to be good. Sin distorts the good and leverages it for evil.

So understand that God knows your frame. He designed you. He knows what you are capable of, for both good and evil. He knows that if you allow His nature and life to consume you, every part of you will shine with glory and goodness!

When we separate the good from God, bad things start to happen. God looked at us and called us "good" when He created us, and nothing can change that. His words are eternal and still vibrate through space and time, constantly stating His opinion of us: "Good." The entrance of sin into the world distorted this good, distracted us from this good, but did not and could not destroy this good.

When Jesus rose from the dead, He sent a tidal wave of life raising up every person on the planet who would trust in Him. And the good lying dormant in us was re-created as we became new people. Not with a goodness of our own, but a goodness that is of Him. The Christ-life.

The Real Painter

A crowd pressed against the rope barrier that kept the sweaty huddle of tourists from touching her face. Sunlight filled the museum and cast a crisp, clear light onto the massive Renaissance paintings that covered the walls around them. People in the crowd jostled for selfies and tried to push their way forward to take a photo of the portrait.

Her face was still frozen in that mysterious half smile as she watched the mayhem. The normal daily streams of people came to see her. She felt sorry for them. No one seemed to enjoy the other beautiful art that adorned the hall. But they were overcome by a frantic obsession to get a quick glimpse of her face. She watched them, entertained by the embarrassing contortions they made to get their phones into the right position.

She had always been a painting that found it difficult to hold on to memories for very long. But last night, she had heard a story that had turned her world upside down, and she fought hard to keep it as her dominant thought. Lost somewhere in the fog of her past was the true identity of her painter. She had always imagined the artist as a distracted genius at best or a disappointed perfectionist at worst. And the latter thought had tormented her mind for years. The fear that she was the least of his paintings was a belief she couldn't shake.

That was until she heard a different story about him. She reeled under this new knowledge that the painter had not only liked her but had actually seemed to love her. So much so that he gave everything he had to get her back.

This new story had unlocked faint memories, and flickers of joy flashed into her mind. Remnants of long-lost moments with the painter. An image had come to her today of the painter sitting on a simple wooden chair in front of her. He smiled and seemed to have no other agenda but to just look at her face. And his gaze seemed to reach through the centuries and hold her attention even now. His eyes saw her in a way that the frantic crowds could not. It was the unhurried attention of love.

She smiled through the crowd and kept the image of him in her mind. Holding on desperately to this new picture of him that had redefined her existence.

Final Brushstrokes

We are like paintings, and God is like the painter. The painting in our little parable had gotten the identity of the painter all wrong. And so do we. Sometimes we must have our image of God re-painted. Re-formed. That's what this book is about.

Maybe you grew up in church like me and you've picked up some wrong ideas about God along the way. Or maybe you don't know if you believe in God. Maybe you are staring at a blank canvas, unsure of what is true. Either way, God can be known. A friend once told me that "God cannot be known exhaustively, but He can be known accurately." In other words, even though God is limitless and beyond our total comprehension, we can know what is true about Him, and we can reject what is false about Him.

I don't claim to have cornered the market on God's identity, but I do want to talk about some of the true things we can know about Him. What does the Bible tell us God is like? We will explore these claims. Who are some of the people throughout history who experienced this God? We will hear their stories. These will help paint an accurate portrait of this God who loves us.

In the next chapter, I will tell the story of one the most important people in the twentieth century. A man who was searching for love and eventually found it.

Discussion Questions

1. Why do you think we have such a difficult time accepting God's love even if we've heard the phrase "God loves you" over and over?

2. In what ways do you think your view of God has been incomplete? Is there a certain area that you have emphasized while forgetting another?

3. How do you think the love of God affects all His other attributes?

4. In the parable "Getting Her Back," the painter goes to great lengths to rescue his lost treasure. In what way has God done that for you?

Chapter 2

"THE LION"—
GOD OF JOY

Finding Home

His train arrived at midday. He stood on the platform for a moment to take it in. He was really here. He had finally arrived at the place he had longed for and worked so hard to reach.

If this was Oxford, though, it was a little underwhelming. Dull buildings surrounded the typical English train station. The smell of diesel exhaust from the passing delivery trucks mixed with the scent of fish and chips wafting from the pub across the street.

He picked up his luggage and began to walk with the boundless energy and optimism of youth. He was lost in his thoughts of all the things he could be here. Could he finally break free from his overbearing father? Could he find a showcase for his great mind?

It was a while before he noticed that the streets on which he walked were growing more dreary and dilapidated with each step. Was this really Oxford? Drab houses and dirty lanes? Where were the dreamy spires and green lawns? It was not until he reached the countryside that he turned back to see the ancient university in the distance behind him.

In his excitement, he had taken a wrong turn out of the train station and walked in the opposite direction of the city, always expecting to round the next bend in the road and come upon beautiful Oxford. With sore feet, he began the long walk back.

This little error would prove to be prophetic, for Oxford would hold more than one surprise for him.

Instead of entering that great medieval city with fresh legs and energy to spare, he arrived disheveled and a bit embarrassed. He hailed a taxi. "Would you be kind enough to take me to the nearest lodgings?" he said breathlessly.

Shortly after, he was deposited at a small inn on Mansfield Road and ushered into a shared room with an odd Welshman. The next morning, he turned onto Holywell Street and began the cold, brisk walk to the hall at Oriel College.

This was it! Walking the streets the greatest minds in England had haunted. To hear lectures echo off stone walls that had stood for more than five hundred years. His dream to one day earn a chair as a fellow of Oxford would become his obsession.

He was of a literary bent, described as "a man of letters." He loved literature. He devoted every waking moment to study and reading. In his free time, he either wrote letters to his friends and family or worked on his poetry. He had learned Greek, Latin, and Italian in order to read the classics in their original languages. All his vigorous study had prepared him for this moment: to take the entrance exam for Oxford.

With cold hands and a wind-chapped face, he stepped into the packed hall at Oriel. Clive Staples Lewis couldn't have known it that day, but that place and the people he would meet there would change not only his life but the lives of millions around the world.

Sensing Joy

Jack, Lewis's nickname for himself, passed the entrance exam to Oxford and had only just begun getting his feet wet in his studies when the Great War began. He served in combat, was injured, and after his convalescence went back to school.

But now he struggled. The war was a brief but horrific interlude in his life. He saw unbearable things. His closest friend in his company was killed. While raised in a Christian home in Ireland, he'd been brought up on the teachings of the church, but early on he had decided God couldn't be real. His mother had died when he was only nine years old. He remembered praying that God would save her life, but his desperate request seemed to have fallen on deaf ears.

His childhood angst at God had turned into full-blown atheism as a young man. And if his journey away from God needed any more help, his traumatic experiences in the war had seared his mind.

When he returned from the war, his time at Oxford became a flurry of activity. He had new friends, demanding studies, poetry to write, and ever-present financial problems that kept him dangling on the edge of poverty.

But he was smart, and he knew it. His mind often raced past other students. If he was confident in his intellectual prowess, he was even more confident in his worldview. The idea of God was laughable to him now. He saw a simple, material world with nothing supernatural about it.

But there were weak spots in his armor. First was his deep desire to follow the crowd. He chased every new intellectual fashion, only to abandon it for a more "sensible" one months later. The absurdity of this was not lost on him.

Second, his love of all things "high" and beautiful never left. His childhood obsession with Norse mythology stayed close to his heart, though this would have been an embarrassing admission to his new friends.

He was still struck by a feeling he could not escape and couldn't fully explain. Most of his friends didn't have the wisdom or ability to even name it. He was struggling with the pangs of a deep and divine joy calling him to God.

The Signposts of Joy

As Lewis found, each and every one of us has an inconsolable longing. For some personalities, it feels more pronounced. For others, it is buried deep beneath the busyness of life. Whether we are aware of it or not, it is there.

Lysa TerKeurst summed it up succinctly in the title of her book *Made to Crave*. God designed us to long for Him. This longing, when misplaced and misused, becomes our worst enemy. But good news! When we direct this longing toward God, it becomes the greatest gift in life, leading to complete fulfillment.

Lewis described joy in a unique way. He spoke of it not as an end unto itself but as a means to an end. Modern thinking tends to make joy (or happiness) both the compass and the destination. Are you not happy with your job? Quit! What matters is that you "reach" happiness! Not happy with your marriage? Quit! What matters is that you "reach" happiness! Our culture tells us that joy is supposed to be both the moral meter by which we gauge success and the ultimate goal of life.

Lewis connected joy not with the frills of happiness but the deep pangs of desire.

> Joy is distinct not only from pleasure in general but even from aesthetic pleasure. It must have the stab, the pang, the inconsolable longing.[1]

He gets beneath the shallow feeling of happiness to the underlying motivation for life. It's not just about happiness but fulfillment.

There has never been a time when personal happiness has been given as much weight in decision-making as now. It seems that almost every talking head in pop culture repeats the mantra, "Do what makes you happy!"

The question is, do we even know what makes us happy? Sure, most of us can name the things that give us pleasure: "Going hiking makes me happy," or "Getting exercise every day really helps my mood." These things are wonderful, of course, but in the long term, are they going to make us fundamentally happy? Such "life hacks" are helpful for a time, but their benefits have an expiration date. The weekend hike always ends, and then comes Monday morning. The endorphins from our workout dissipate as we reengage the difficulties of life.

Joy must be something more than just happiness. Lewis says that joy is actually a deep *longing*. Our moments of happiness and pleasure

are hints of what we long for. The hike and the exercise are enjoyable
not because they themselves are the source of joy, but because there is
something greater and deeper behind them.

There is a God who created beautiful trails and the endorphins
that surge through our bodies. And we can actually break through
the veil and see the One who gave them to us! Joy is meant to be an
indicator that this is possible. In other words, joy isn't the ultimate
end, but God created it to draw us to Himself. Because He is the
ultimate end.

> All Joy reminds. It is never a possession, always a
> desire for something longer ago or further away or
> still "about to be."[2]

In a later chapter speaking of the thrill of joy, Lewis says:

> Its very existence presupposes that you desire not it
> but something other and outer. [3]

God gave us not only a desire for Him but also beautiful and good
things that remind us of Him. In the end, all those signs and feelings
and desires are meant to lead us to the true destination: God Himself.
Again, Lewis describes this journey:

> It [joy] was valuable only as a pointer to something
> other and outer. While that other was in doubt,
> the pointer naturally loomed large in my thoughts.

When we are lost in the woods the sight of a sign-post is a great matter. He who first sees it cries, "Look!" The whole party gathers round and stares. But when we have found the road and are passing signposts every few miles, we shall not stop and stare.[4]

The Ski Chalet

If the pangs of joy are signposts pointing us to God, sometimes we can get stuck dwelling on them. We are surrounded by temptations and distractions in this age of information.

I was on YouTube one day and clicked my way to a Sotheby's video of a ten-million-dollar mountain chalet. It had "ski-in and ski-out access" to one of the most exclusive ski resorts in the world. It had a massive, heated pool. The living room looked like a palace with giant windows overlooking the snowy mountains. Everything about this home was a dream.

Two minutes into the video I had a rapid succession of thoughts:

Curiosity: "There are houses like this?"

Awe: "This place is ridiculous!"

Desire: "It would be so cool to stay there!"

Lust: "Actually, forget that—I want to own this place ... NOW!"

Disappointment: "I don't have ten million dollars."

Jealousy: "Why are other people allowed to own that place if I can't?"

Comparison: "How successful are the people who stay here? And what did I do wrong?"

Scheming: "Maybe I could get it together and become a millionaire."

Embarrassment: "I'm watching a video of a ten-million-dollar house and trying to figure out how I can buy it?"

Resignation: "Well, that was interesting. Sigh. Back to real life."

I wonder what God was thinking during this two-minute train wreck of mine? Was He laughing or crying? A bit of both, I would imagine!

Later, I thought about why I had taken such a quick descent into jealousy and lust—over a house. Then I remembered something: I was made for more. I was made for heaven. I am an exile in a foreign country. I am homesick. And every once in a while, I run into something that reminds me of home. Something beautiful. Something grand. My sin-tainted heart makes a mess of the moment. I take the wrong turn. And the very thing that was meant to remind me of who I am makes me forget who I am.

That mansion is a faint imitation of the real grandeur I was designed for. Every desire you have is meant to remind you that God is your true desire.

So, when my heart desires a lesser thing, I remind my heart of the greater thing. I remember the unlimited treasure that I have in knowing Jesus.

Giving In

There were cracks in Lewis's armor. For all his resistance against God, he had a weak spot for joy. Deep joy. The joy that aches in your belly when you see something truly beautiful. You reach for it but can't grasp it. You try to re-create the same feeling the next day, only to find it missing. This haunted Lewis.

He began to do what he always did to find answers: he read books and talked deeply with his friends.

One of these fateful talks with his friend Owen Barfield went late into the night. Barfield was a genius on par with Lewis who could go toe-to-toe with him in mental jousting. He also happened to be a Christian. Sitting in Lewis's rooms at Magdalen College, they talked about God, truth, and beauty. Some points began to connect for Lewis, and his defenses against God suffered a great blow.

Not too long after this, other friends joined him for a walk. J. R. R. Tolkien and Hugo Dyson strolled with him under the trees of Addison's Walk, a trail on the Magdalen College grounds. Lewis raised a challenge to his friends: "What separates Christianity from any other myth? After all, there are other stories about a god 'saving' his people."

His friends responded with an idea that changed his life. "Yes, Christianity is a myth," they said. "But it is the only true myth."

Suddenly, he realized that the Norse mythology he loved was never the real source of the joy he felt. It was God. Every good and beautiful myth was simply pointing to the one true "myth." This was a devastating blow to Lewis's atheism. Now it was only a matter of time before he would fully give in. For God had won the battle for his mind, and his heart would soon follow.

His conversion to Christianity came in short order. He wrote about the moment this happened, in his autobiography:

> You must picture me alone in that room in Magdalen, night after night, feeling, whenever my mind lifted even for a second from my work, the steady, unrelenting approach of Him whom I so earnestly desired not to meet. That which I greatly feared had at last come upon me. In the Trinity Term of 1929 I gave in, and admitted that God was God, and knelt and prayed: perhaps, that night, the most dejected and reluctant convert in all England.[5]

G. K. Chesterton said, "Joy, which is the small publicity of the pagan, is the gigantic secret of the Christian."[6] True Christianity, the giving up of yourself to God, is perfect joy. Romans 14:17 says, "For the kingdom of God is not a matter of eating and drinking but of righteousness and peace and joy in the Holy Spirit."

Isn't it interesting that something as vast and overwhelming as the kingdom of God could be described with only three words? It really is that simple: When we get God, we get what

He has—and He has a lot of righteousness, peace, and joy. A never-ending supply of it!

This is what drew Lewis in. It won both his mind and his heart. This is divine wisdom: that God is our true source of joy and the real object of every deep desire we have.

The God of Color

Our mind will come up with a thousand reasons not to honor God. And most of them are perfectly rational. Things like, "I can't tell that person the truth—it will hurt him!" or "I don't need to pay my taxes—the government will just misuse my money!" These justifications may or may not be true, but no matter how much we wiggle and dance around the issue, God's truth is still there, unchanged. "You shall not steal. You shall not bear false witness" (Ex. 20:15–16a).

We know deep down that His way is best, but our sinful nature wants its own way. We build up mental defenses against God, the two most effective being busyness and noise. So we buzz around with the music cranked and a phone in our face. We fill every space, terrified of the silence.

But inevitably our vigilance wanes and His patient pursuit prevails. We find ourselves in a still moment, and before we know it, He begins to speak. Maybe not in sentences but in a little prick of the conscience or a rush of unexpected joy. It is God breaking through our defenses and getting our attention.

We were made to be in relationship with Him. We are dying when we are disconnected from Him. So, in His mercy, He never stops pursuing us. This is a matter life and death for us, so He will use whatever is necessary to get our attention.

This happened to me recently. I went to an art museum to do some writing because I needed some inspiration.

I decided that when I saw the first piece of art that really moved me, I would sit down and begin to write. I'm a bit of a history nerd, so I went straight for the antiquities. I saw great Roman statues and beautiful Greek vases from 1500 BC. I walked past a massive Egyptian sarcophagus. These are things that normally get me pretty pumped, but I felt no spark of ideation. Nothing.

> **When we get God, we get what He has—and He has a lot of righteousness, peace, and joy.**

So I moved on to my favorite artistic time period, the Renaissance. Here was my happy place! European majesty in deep hues of red and brown. But this time, the paintings that normally would have captured my attention felt lifeless. Even the paintings of Christ seemed distant that day. It felt a bit odd, but as I passed painting after painting, I didn't feel what I'd gone there to feel.

After a while, with tired feet and feeling a little silly for even trying this experiment, I turned to leave. The way out led me through the Impressionist paintings. I glanced casually around and then stopped in my tracks.

The painting before me was so simple. It was a scene of a man reading a book in what looked like a Parisian park. Compared to the darker paintings I had just seen, this one leaped off the wall with vibrant color. It demanded my attention. The man in the painting was sitting on a chair in the shade with his back to the observer. And the sun shone behind boxed orange trees onto a thick patch of vibrant flowers. It was a bright and beautiful painting. (It was *The Orange Trees* by Gustave Caillebotte, 1878.)

I felt God say to me, "Jack, I am the God of color."

In that moment I realized something: I'm always trying to find God in the stern and serious things when He is actually waiting for me in the joyful things too.

James tells us, "Every good gift and every perfect gift is from above, coming down from the Father of lights" (v. 1:17a). The Father of *lights*! The Father of color. The gift giver. The joyful painter.

Never forget that God is having fun. And He wants to bring you into that joy! Is He there in your suffering? Yes. Is He the almighty God who thunders? Yes. But He's also the God who made elephants and monkeys. Sunsets and peacocks. Honey and strawberries. There is more to Him than we know, and He desires for us to experience every bit of it.

Finding Hope

The soaring harmonies of the choir filled the chapel at Magdalen College. Wooden benches creaked and feet shuffled as a few late worshippers took their seats. It was a small but truly beautiful church. Lewis breathed deeply of the chilly air that filled the stone chapel, and it reminded him of an older world. He opened his eyes and took in the light that burst through the stained glass.

He thought of *northerness*, the piercing beauty of the Nordic sagas he had loved all his life. They had a new meaning to him now. It had been Christ all along, hiding within each story. Christ, finally breaking through and guiding him to this moment. Had someone told him thirty years ago that he would one day be sitting here in this chapel as a worshipper, he would have laughed. Yet here he was.

After his conversion, Lewis had originally decided that his would be a private devotion with no church attendance required. Surely shutting yourself in a room with shelves full of the devotional writers and a healthy dose of prayer was all a new Christian needed. He soon found the folly in this thinking and made a commitment to public worship.

He attended college chapel on most weekday mornings and the Anglican church near his home in Headington on Sundays. Mostly, he went out of faithfulness and obedience, not because he had grand spiritual experiences at church. But this day was different. He came with a desperation he hadn't felt in quite some time. He was tired. Frustrated. Worried even, which wasn't like him.

His brother was missing again on what could only be another drinking binge. Lewis was no longer a student, and the workload for his job as a tutor was as great as it had ever been. He worked himself to the bone at school and then went home to a sort of domestic tyranny.

He lived with the mother of Paddy Moore, his closest friend in his company during the Great War. They had made a commitment to one another that, should either of them perish, the other would take care of his family. Paddy died. So Lewis, then a twenty-two-year-old college student with almost no money, vowed to financially support Paddy's mother and younger sister. Over the years since then, Mrs. Moore had become a mother figure to Lewis, and Paddy's sister had become like a sister to him.

Mrs. Moore was now in her eighties. In her younger years, she'd been a pleasant person, but in her old age, she had become nearly intolerable in her daily demands. From the time Lewis awoke until the time he went to bed, he catered to her every preference and coped with her petty complaining. He bore this suffering with all the love and patience he could muster.

Making matters worse, his work life was no longer a tranquil retreat but a source of frustration. By this point, he had written several books. They had sold well and met with critical acclaim. However, despite all the success he had enjoyed as an author, his career as a medieval scholar and educator had all but ground to a halt.

Since his mid-twenties, he'd been a tutor at Magdalen College, a job that came with a suffocating workload. For years, he had seen his colleagues, some with half his talent, go on to become department chairs of prominent Oxford colleges. Yet his name got passed over time and time again. It was no secret that his success as a popular author (and even worse, a *Christian* author) had made him fall out of favor with the voting faculty.

He closed his eyes for the final prayer of the service and took a deep breath. Suddenly, he felt it: another world. The world of talking beasts he had been building since childhood. He smelled the cool, crisp mountain air and heard the crunch of snow underfoot. There was a lamppost standing amid the snow-laden pines.

He smiled, and the scene quickly changed in his mind. He saw a great lion staring at him with piercing eyes. He felt love all around him. Christ was here. He was with him. Joy was possible even in these frustrating times.

As he stood to leave the chapel, he made a quick mental note: *Start working on that wardrobe idea tonight.*

Losing Joy

Ten years later, Lewis sat in an armchair in a space in his home he called the "common room." One of the walls of the small rectangular room was lined with shelves stuffed full of books, many of them written by him. A desk stood by the window that looked out onto the back gardens. He stared into the sky with blank eyes. Joy was gone.

Earlier that day, his wife had died right in front of him in her bed. The fiery American who had stormed into his life with two boys and turned his world upside down. The woman who had stayed up late into the night with him as they spoke of life, love, and poetry. The woman he loved ... was gone.

Lewis had spent most of his life as a bachelor. Because of his career and the ever-increasing demand of caring for Mrs. Moore, he had missed out on the domestic bliss that many of his friends had found. But late in life, God had surprised him with the gift that was Joy Davidman.

She was brilliant, funny, compassionate, and wise. She lit up the room with her charisma. She went head-to-head with him in dialectic swordplay. She helped him give birth to what many consider to be his greatest work of fiction, *Till We Have Faces*. She brought her two sons, David and Douglas, into his life. Never having had children of his own, Lewis had taken to the boys and had started to fill the role of father in their life. He remembered Joy's smile as he had patiently talked to the boys about whatever topic was on their minds.

And now she was gone. The pain was so deep that he could barely breathe as he stared into the garden. Joy had revived it, tending it with a feminine care that seemed to bring out the best in every flower and plant. The weight on his chest increased. Finally, feeling that he could bear it no longer, he stood from the chair and burst out the front door in a tearful rage. The only thing he could do was walk.

How could God have done this? How could He give a gift so wonderful and take her away so soon, after only eight years of knowing her? Wouldn't it have been better for him to be alone than to know love for such a short time only to have it ripped away from him? He knew the answers, but he smothered them with strong hands. He let his rage boil over and hurled accusations at God with the precision and cruelty that only someone with his mind could manage.

After walking in a blind fury for more than an hour, he found himself at the top of a hill. It was a place he had been many times with friends on afternoon rambles. The last time he'd been here ... had been with her. It felt like a stab in his side. The realization that there would be no more of these moments in the days to come as he stumbled upon a hundred other places he had shared with her in Oxford. Should he just leave?

Leave. What if he really left? Left it all. Left this God he had spent his whole adult life defending. The one he had sacrificed his academic career for, only to be left alone on this hilltop.

Before he could finish his thought, the presence of God rushed up the hill at him like a violent gale of wind but stopped short of his face like a whisper. It surrounded him like a shield and stood watch over him as he wept. Then the whisper spoke: "I love her more than you do. The joy of having her was worth the pain of losing her. Joy is not gone. She is with Me. And I am with you."

Lewis walked back down the hill and made his way back to the Kilns. "I must get back to the boys."

Final Brushstrokes

The years before Lewis's conversion were all about searching. He sought to find fulfillment for this deep longing he had. He tried to find it in his favorite mythology and music. He tried to find it in academic and intellectual excellence. But every time he seemed to grasp hold of that magical feeling of joy, it would evaporate through His fingers.

C. S. Lewis's life teaches us that the greatest joys in life are simply signposts pointing us to the ultimate joy that is God. And that when we find Him, we find peace even in deep pain and suffering.

So our portrait of God gets another color: the vibrant hues of joy! We learn that God is not on a mission to stop people from having fun. Actually, the fun begins with Him. We think that worldly pleasures will fulfill us, but they let us down every time. God Himself is the author of everything good, true, and beautiful! And when we find Him, we can truly enjoy the world He made and find an unfading joy that comes from His nature.

Discussion Questions

1. How does Lewis's view of joy as a deeper longing beyond fleeting happiness contrast with today's emphasis on immediate gratification? How can we prioritize true joy in the midst of these external pressures?

2. While Lewis experienced success as a writer, he also endured painful loss and challenges throughout his life. How did understanding God as the ultimate source of joy help him in these times?

3. Just like my story about the ski chalet, what are some "signposts of joy" that you have mistaken for the destination itself? What are some moments when you have forgotten who and what these good things were pointing to?

4. In what ways have you experienced God as the God of color, fun, and creativity? Or has the attribute of God's joy been difficult for you to imagine or connect with?

Chapter 3

"THE BISHOP"— GOD OF HOLINESS

Invitation

He had come to Milan for opportunities. A prodigious public speaker, he had been tapped to become the government's mouthpiece in northern Italy. But he had other reasons for coming here. He had long had an affinity for all things beautiful, especially women. And Milan was a place of infinite possibility, both for his career and for his desires.

His gift as an orator earned him quick fame in a city that loved big ideas and eloquent speech. He became entranced by the sights and sounds of this city that seemed to never sleep.

Sleep. That was for the stuffy religious souls who didn't know how to really live. How could he sleep when there was so much to enjoy? Truth be told, he wanted to sleep but couldn't. He found himself tossing and turning through the small hours of the night. With every dizzying day and cheap thrill came a dull coldness. Soon, the darker side of the city began to leer at him.

His hometown—Hippo Regius, a coastal city in modern-day Algeria—was a small, quiet place, and to his surprise he began to actually miss those simple days in the Carthaginian countryside. He remembered how, just months before, he had pined for the city life. It had indeed dazzled him so far, to be sure.

But today was different. He felt a darkness pressing in as he walked the streets that cold morning. He couldn't shake it this time: that cold loneliness that seemed to seep out of every alley and haunt him. As he walked the streets that Sunday morning, he heard the familiar sound of church bells and the deep chorus of men in robes. The sound terrified him. He had left that foolishness long ago for higher thought. Early in his education, he'd begun to see the holes in Christianity. He could not accept its hypocrisy, its tyranny. He picked up his pace down the lonely street.

"Augustine!" called a strong voice. "Is that you?"

He turned and saw a young man his age. His frame was impressive, even in a brown robe, and his face was warm and inviting on that cold street. The young man stood just outside the church door that Augustine had hurried past.

"Who are you?" Augustine said, not unkindly.

"Grivelli!" the man replied. "Alexander Grivelli! I heard you speak on the piazza two weeks ago. You have a gift, that's for certain. Although," he said with a smile, "I disagreed on a few of the finer points. Would you come in and join us? It is a warm place for a cold morning."

Augustine's first reaction was embarrassment. He knew there had probably been priests who had heard his speech, but to look one in the eye was another thing. He had taken a few not-so-subtle jabs at the church during his talk—in front of a cathedral, no less! He was suddenly self-conscious. He felt naked. This priest must have heard of his reputation. And for the first time in a long time, he felt guilt.

"Come quickly," Alexander said, rubbing his hands together. "Mass is about to begin!"

Augustine was good at saying "no," but for a reason he couldn't quite explain, he felt that Alexander's invitation had no strings attached but was something like pure charity. Before he could talk himself out of it, he was halfway through the church door.

Defining Holiness

In our culture, the word *holiness* has become as distant and arcane to us as some far-off tribe.

When we try to conjure a definition of holiness, we usually get a few images. Maybe we think of moral purity. Things like not lying or cursing or no sex before marriage. And those are fair responses. But they're a bit like holding up a bottle of water when asked to explain a waterfall. Holiness is something altogether higher than just following the rules. Though holiness is never less than moral standards, it is always more than mere morality.

The definition of the Hebrew word translated as *holy* means "set-apartness."[1] Another way to say this would be "other" or someone who is different than anyone we've ever seen. Only God is completely other. Every created being, although unique, is at least similar to others within its race or species. Zebras are similar to horses but still different. Humans come in all shapes and sizes, but they are still all humans.

God has no other similar Gods around Him. He is utterly singular. He stands alone, above, beyond, apart from all of us. From everything. This is where the concept of holiness really begins: in God's complete transcendence. *Holiness* first describes someone's nature and position, and only then can it go on to describe moral characteristics.

In fact, God's moral purity is a direct result of His otherness. There is *no one* who is morally perfect except Him. There is no one as wise or good or loving as Him. And these moral attributes are not only perfect but also so intense as to be more than we can bear to look upon. Unimaginable goodness, purity, uprightness, and love—this is what holiness is. Not just purity or goodness, but purity and goodness that is completely singular and unmatched in all the universe.

The amazing thing is that we are called to partake of this holiness! How? How on earth can *we* be holy? This is a big question. It is one we will explore in this chapter.

Experiencing Holiness

Often, we are just trying to open the "bottled water" of morality, while Christ stands amid a waterfall of glory, inviting us in. We want to start with a moral ethic that works its way to God, but Christianity starts with a moral God who works Himself to us. A God who surges toward us with terrible power and love.

Christ has no interest in just changing your life. He *wants* your life. This is not semantics. These really are two completely different worldviews. One says, "Jesus makes my life better." The other says, "Jesus *is* my life. And because He's the only one that truly matters, I must die. He must live."

Graham Cooke says it this way with his cheeky British humor: "Jesus dealt with your sin once and for all. And when he died you died ... [God is] not trying to fix you, [He] killed you off instead."[2]

> I have been crucified with Christ. It is no longer I
> who live, but Christ who lives in me. And the life I
> now live in the flesh I live by faith in the Son of God,
> who loved me and gave himself for me. (Gal. 2:20)

Jesus wants His resurrection life to make you a new creation. Totally new. Not improved. Not "elevated" or "enlightened." New. Brand new! But you cannot resurrect a living thing. You must die to be resurrected.

Wrestling with God

Augustine paced the floor of a comfortable country house just outside Milan.

His entire adult life had been marked by personal freedom. He did what he wanted when he wanted. He didn't realize how much he liked that kind of life until this moment. So why was God asking him to give it up?

With the chill of the early spring hanging in his room, he felt a shiver of anger run up his spine. There must be some sort of compromise. Why would God be so rigid? Wasn't He good? If He was good, then why did this hurt so much? And where was He right now? Wasn't He supposed to be the comforter?

Not many months before, Augustine had gone into that church and heard the bishop preach. Time after time since then, he'd returned to hear the bishop's words, which were like words he had never heard before. In Bishop Ambrose, he had finally found a man who was not just a Christian but an intellectual. Yet his intellect wasn't one of cold pride but of warm hospitality. In Ambrose, Augustine saw what he had always missed in the Scriptures: the purity of love and the power of God to transform any life.

Week after week, month after month, this onslaught of truth had moved him to a place of both joy and misery. He had finally accepted that the doctrines of Christianity were true. Yet here he was, fighting this inner turmoil. What was wrong? Was there another step to be taken? He knew the answers deep in his heart, but it seemed there was something surging under his skin that would not let go of the fight.

His great intellect was locked in a desperate struggle. He had always been able to solve problems by throwing himself fully into them. He'd never failed to come to a clear conclusion. But today, his mind would make false starts, sputter, and then take wrong turns. He would emerge with what he thought was a mental victory, only to have his legs knocked from under him. At the end of this ordeal, he felt like some great, injured animal trying to get to its feet.

This problem was more complex than even his erudite mind was capable of handling. He had finally found his match in God. Fervor turned to exasperation. Then, like a drowning man reaching the surface and gulping air, his fear changed to peace.

He had reached the place of simple surrender. No matter how painful it was to let go of his sins, he knew it was the only way to be healed. He must give in.

His mind turned to something that had happened earlier in the day. He had received a travel-worn visitor at the house. To Augustine's shock, the man had told him a story of two men who had left their lives of privilege to follow

Christ. They had even given up the young women they were betrothed to in order to join a monastery and devote their lives to prayer.

Remembering that story now, it struck a nerve in Augustine, and he began to weep. Whether they were tears of grief or joy, he could not discern, but one thing was clear: the most important choice of his life was before him. Would he choose Christ Jesus as Lord, or nothing at all? Life or death?

With that in mind, he stepped outside into the sunlight ready to face his deepest fear.

The Death Blow

Christianity is an invitation to experience the surging power of God's life. Jesus doesn't want to just change us ... He wants to resurrect us! But first, we must talk about the unpleasant thing that comes before resurrection: death. Not physical death. But the figurative death of dying to self that Christ invites us to.

This death to your former self (the one that existed before you came to Christ) is an unusual kind of dying. It is not like the death of a loved one but more like the death of a tyrant. There is no grieving at the graveside. There is actually *rejoicing* that the old life is gone and a new one has been born.

> For whoever would save his life will lose it, but whoever loses his life for my sake and the gospel's will save it. (Mark 8:35)

Therefore, if anyone is in Christ, he is a new creation.
The old has passed away; behold, the new has come.
(2 Cor. 5:17)

Some have wondered, "If Jesus died for us, then why do we have to die to ourselves?"

Jesus died so that we *could* "die." We were separated from God in our sin, unable to be in relationship with Him. Christ came to die in our place so that if we received Him, we would be made right with God. We are washed from our sins by His blood and now stand in His righteousness.

It is that simple. But it is simple in the way that an atomic explosion is simple. The concept is beautifully uncomplicated yet deeply disruptive. The Lord's righteousness is not a passive theory but a violent reality, never letting you stay comfortable in sin and always holding grace up as the standard.

Our culture looks at the simplicity of the gospel and mistakes it for something negotiable or peripheral, but the good news of Jesus is all or nothing! It is the wonderful gift of love, but we often forget that it is not just one gift among a thousand similar ones. The gospel is completely singular. There are no other alternatives by which we can experience the life of God.

What Augustine experienced is what many people fear about Christianity: the demand that we lay everything down for God. This is the dying I'm referring to. Our relationships, our time, our money, our jobs. I don't mean we must lay them down as in literally leave them. Usually, all we must do is say, "God, they are Yours completely. I am Yours completely. Whatever You tell me to do, I will do."

Being saved is less about bringing Jesus into our lives and more about Him rescuing us out of our lives and bringing us into His.

I remember seeing the images of people stranded on their rooftops in New Orleans after Hurricane Katrina devastated their city. The rescuers didn't sit down with them on the roof and hang out for a coffee. They put them on a boat or helicopter and got them out of there!

Before we are born again, we are stuck in a life we weren't designed to live. We were created to be in perfect union with God. And every day we live estranged from Him, we are fighting against our eternal purpose, and the waters are rising around us. This life we are called to die to is a false life, a half life. And Jesus came to literally rescue us from it.

I love the way Todd White puts it: "So all God is asking you to do is to give up something you were never created to be."[3]

Our enemy is in an information war, trying to convince us that we like this half life. After all, sin is fun! At least for a short time. But sin is fun in the way that doing heroin is fun. Short-term pleasure, long-term pain.

Jesus died for us so we could experience the glorious gift of God's presence. But how can we accept this gift while holding on to our old life? Our hearts are occupied, unable to receive the gift.

This dying to self is swift. It is total and it is simple. As simple as saying yes to God. And, by His grace, making a decision in your heart to make Him Lord. He cannot be your Savior if you won't let Him be Your Lord. The God who has the power to save you is the God whose power you must humble yourself before. The God who loves you with an everlasting love wants to consume every part of your life with this love.

Death is quick. His life is eternal.

The sunlight hit his face as he made his way to the garden. The wind brought the scent of evergreens and fresh water. The beauty surrounding him felt at odds with the ugly war in his heart.

Augustine was still shedding tears from a place so deep in him that he could not name it. The decision stood before him, and he realized that no change in scenery would alter it. It seemed that all around him there were unseen forces in a desperate battle for his soul. One side terrified of defeat and the other joyfully expectant of a new life that was soon to be born.

He heard a faint sound. He stopped to strain his ears. It sounded like children singing. It reminded him of pure days and simple truths. After the inner turmoil of the recent hours, it felt like cool water on a parched tongue.

He looked all around but could see no children. Their song grew more intense in his ears with an almost taunting quality. He heard it so clearly that there could be no question of misunderstanding what they were singing: "Take up and read! Take up and read!"

It was a melody from a child's game, yet it had all the terrifying qualities of the handwriting on the wall in King Belshazzar's palace. It was a clear message.

He ran back inside, and his gaze fell on a leather book. It was St. Paul's letter to the Romans. Again the song rang in his ears: "Take up and read! Take up and read!"

Feeling more than a little foolish, he picked up the book and opened it. His eyes landed on a passage that struck like lightning:

Not in orgies and drunkenness, not in sexual immorality and sensuality, not in quarreling and jealousy. But put on the Lord Jesus Christ, and make no provision for the flesh, to gratify its desires. (vv. 13:13–14)

In that moment, Augustine gave in. The strong hand of God had not let him go and had pulled him in with the gentleness of a child's song. This demand of God was actually an invitation. Augustine knew it was a privilege to give everything to Him and an honor to lay it all down in order to take up something greater.

Little did Augustine know that his decision would shape the world.

The King's Demand

Jesus has a total demand on our lives, not because of what He has done for us, but simply because of who He is.

When He called the disciples to follow Him, He had yet to go to the cross on their behalf. He was simply calling them because He is the eternal King of Kings. He calls us in the same way. Life and death hang in the balance of our response to this invitation. The only appropriate response to someone so high and great is complete surrender. This total demand on our lives is grace. It is love. Without it, we cannot even hope to experience real joy or life.

If God didn't demand our total surrender, it would mean that He didn't actually love us. In other words, if He allowed us to choose both

Him and the world, He would not be loving us at all. It is His love that makes His demand absolute.

That statement may rub us the wrong way, I know. Our culture doesn't like to hear about humans demanding submission. We have experienced and heard about all sorts of abuse. But God is not a toxic abuser—He is a good and loving God. One who is all wise and can be trusted. (He proved this by dying on the cross for us.) He cannot *desire* anything toward us that He won't work for our ultimate good. So, surrendering completely to Him is just another way of saying you are surrendering to love, joy, and peace!

Augustine understood this total demand from God. That's why he struggled so much with his conversion. He lived in a time when making a public profession for Christ cost something. He knew it was going to cost him his reputation and his position of ease as a government orator. He knew it would cost him his pet sins and lusts. This is why he weighed the decision so heavily. There was no mistaking it: Christ was demanding everything.

> When Christ calls you, there is no "*but first.*" It is as simple as saying Yes or No. Following Him or walking away.

In our modern culture of individualism, it is harder for us to process this demand. We are steeped in a tradition of personal "freedom." We know there are certain rules we shouldn't break, mainly felonies, but pretty much anything else goes. (And hey, if you're willing to go to prison, even the felonies are yours for the taking!) Our society really boils everything down to, "What do you need to do in order to be happy?"

If you are married and you want another woman, our culture responds with a resounding, "Go for it. If that's the life you want, take it. Will there be consequences? Sure! Your kids will experience trauma and the mother of your children will be estranged to you. But that's just the price you have to pay to get the life you want. It's not necessarily wrong—it's just what it is. So long as you're willing to live with the consequences of your decisions, everything is open to you. Do what you want!"

I say all that for one purpose: you may not realize it, but even if you were raised in a Christian home, you have been deeply affected by this kind of thinking.

So, when Christ comes and says, "Follow Me," we respond, "Yes, Lord! But first ..."

When Christ calls you, there is no "*but first.*" It is as simple as saying Yes or No. Following Him or walking away.

This offends our modern sensibilities because it is so abrasive and absolute. It leaves no room for dialogue or negotiation. This call from Christ seems to us irrational in the truest sense of the word. It doesn't take into account any of our rationalizations or commonsense arguments. But the truth still stands: you don't argue with a king.

Dietrich Bonhoeffer said it well in *The Cost of Discipleship*:

> Costly grace is the gospel which must be sought again
> and again and again, the gift which must be asked
> for, the door at which a man must knock. Such grace
> is costly because it calls us to follow, and it is grace

because it calls us to follow Jesus Christ. It is costly because it costs a man his life, and it is grace because it gives a man the only true life. It is costly because it condemns sin, and grace because it justifies the sinner. Above all, it is costly because it cost God the life of his Son: "Ye were bought at a price," and what has cost God much cannot be cheap for us. Above all, it is grace because God did not reckon his Son too dear a price to pay for our life, but delivered him up for us. Costly grace is the Incarnation of God.[4]

The Good King

I've got some great news for you: Yes, the King is demanding everything, but He is not just any old king—He is the perfect King. He is the good King. He died on a cross for us. He is the King who has already given what He is demanding from us: everything.

He is the King who can be trusted. He is the King who never makes a mistake. He is the King who will never hurt us.

> The thief comes only to steal and kill and destroy. I came that they may have life and have it abundantly. (John 10:10)

He can never do anything that is not in your best interests. (Even though in the moment it may *feel* like it is not.) Everything He asks from you is so that you can experience His abundant life. If God is saying No right now, it just means that He has a better Yes.

The Greek word behind *abundant* in that sentence literally means "more than is necessary."[5] He wants to give you life, life, and more life! He gives us more joy than we deserve! More peace than we need! Just because He is good. No other reason.

He is asking for all that you can give Him, because He wants to give you all that He is.

The Self-Expression Ethic

I want to talk about one of the greatest barriers to holiness. In a time when virtue is mocked, we see one modern "virtue" holding strong: self-expression. Self-expression has become the great vision of our age. The moral compass of our time. In the eyes of our culture, the greatest sin in this century is to not allow someone to "be" what she decides she wants to be.

This, of course, is entirely selective on the person's part. When it comes to actions that hurt others, like murder or domestic abuse, our culture rightly draws a line and says that these things are absolutely wrong.

Yet when the Bible calls something wrong that the culture has decided is permissible, suddenly truth is relative. "I'll live my truth and you live yours." Well, we can't have it both ways. Either murder is objectively wrong, which implies that there is a set of unchanging moral rules that govern the world, or murder is not wrong, implying that all rules are whatever we make them. There is no middle ground, even though many of us try to pretend there is.

God's prohibitive laws (His noes) are a safeguard that not only keep us from hurting others but also from hurting ourselves through misguided self-expression. (I would add that hurting yourself is a very serious thing when you are created in the image of God.)

Our culture hates to be told no. It's one of the most fundamental affronts to self-indulgent people. So when Christ comes and demands all, they balk. He demands all because He *gives* all. Yet we get so hung up on the lordship demand that we miss out on the treasures He longs to give. But there is no separating the grace of God from His demand for total obedience. They are one and the same.

Christianity undercuts the modern self-expression ethic and sets God's original plan before us. Does God want us to express ourselves? Of course! But He wants you to express your real self. And He is the only one who knows who we were truly made to be. So, in order to become our true selves, we must submit to Him. Then we will learn amazing things about ourselves, because He is an amazing creator!

When we run from Him and decide who we want to be, that is the exact opposite of true self-expression. It is ultimately a form of self-hatred because rejecting His good plan for us works as a slow destruction to our entire being.

Go read the story of Adam and Eve. Look at their life before they chose their own way compared with their life after they chose their own way. Which life would you prefer? Would you choose the one in paradise or the one in misery? Did their self-expression apart from God increase their personal happiness or cause pain and despair?

It was only when Adam and Eve began expressing themselves in their own way separate from God's plan that things started to collapse. God's original plan of "self-expression" was absolutely glorious.

The good news is that the original plan has been restored by Jesus Christ, whom the Bible calls "the last Adam" (1 Cor. 15:45). And when we lay down our old life and begin to follow Him, we find out how magnificent we were intended to be.

Today's version of self-expression is a cheap and shrill perversion of something glorious. In fact, is it directly opposed to truly "finding yourself." The real you is in Jesus. The farther you get from Him, the less you are like you and the more you become a strange thing.

Holiness as Preparation

Personal holiness is the outworking of God's nature in us over the course of time. It is a process that plays out over the length of a lifetime. So that makes the time we have here of utmost importance. This life is our opportunity to choose God among a million other alternatives. Every day, we face decisions on how we will use our time. Will we choose God and His goodness or the way of this age and its distractions?

I've noticed something interesting in our modern "hustle" and "work" culture: non-Christians are often obsessed with time. The millennial entrepreneur movement is a good example of this. Memes and posts abound about always being on "the grind" and "working harder" than everyone else.

The Christian ought to value time in a different way. Yes, we are diligent and give our best to our work. We, like non-Christians, know that time is a finite resource, so we must steward it wisely. But we do it all from a different motivation than the world. The non-Christian uses time. The Christian redeems time.

Non-Christians value time because they believe this is the only chance they have before existence ends. "You only live once" is their motto. Christians value time because this temporal existence is the only chance they have to prepare before life at its fullest really begins.

The non-Christian lives like a great violinist trying to fully perform a solo before the stage collapses. But the Christian lives like a violinist who plays with joy and tunes with care because he knows that one day he will join the real orchestra. Both care about this life, but only the Christian can give it the seriousness it deserves while at the same time enjoying the beauty it gives.

The non-Christian has only the hustle and the grind. The Christian is actually working toward something greater than this world. We have something more than our work—we have God Himself. And the reason our work matters deeply is that it is one of the means by which we can know God more and become like Him. It is a tool in our hands that makes us holy as He is holy and reveals His goodness to the world around us.

Augustine sat at a table covered in manuscripts and letters. The late evening chill blew through the open window as a small fire flickered behind him. He was scribbling away at a piece of parchment when a figure darkened the door.

He stood from the table with a smile on his face and walked over to greet his friend. From the way he welcomed the visitor, an observer would never have known the concerns that pressed on his very soul.

After his conversion, Augustine had returned to Africa hoping to find a secluded piece of land and settle down. He was excited to have a quiet, intellectual life, devoting himself to Christian study and writing. He dreamed of teaching a few students in philosophy and theology, and when he wanted to retire to his study, he could just send them away. This never happened. Upon his return to Hippo, the congregation had physically pulled him down to the altar and demanded that he be their bishop. He could not deny their desperate request. More importantly, he knew he could not deny the call of God. Once again, he had a choice to make: his way or God's way. He chose God's.

He was soon swept up into the current of church life. He attended to the pressing needs of the people, discipled new converts, preached almost daily, and managed the details of church business. This happened while the church was under attack from the outside. Many looked to Augustine to use his rhetorical gifts for the defense of the faith.

Back in Augustine's study, he embraced his friend. "Marcellinus, my brother! What a gift to see your face!"

Marcellinus couldn't help but notice that, although his friend looked much older than when he had last seen him, he had a brighter and deeper joy in his eyes. It was as if Augustine had grown older and younger all at once.

Augustine showed Marcellinus to a set of chairs by the small fireplace. "How are things across the sea?"

Marcellinus sat and looked into the flame as if he were staring into some recent horror. He turned to Augustine with a glimmer of tears in his eyes and shook his head.

"So the reports are true?" Augustine asked gravely.

"Yes. And they are most certainly worse than the faint rumors that have reached the shores of Carthage. I was there. And my heart breaks even to think of it."

"Did they spare the churches?" Augustine asked just above a whisper.

"Well, that is the only hope to be found in the whole affair!" Happiness flashed across Marcellinus's face, then faded into anger. "It was the only place the barbarians wouldn't touch. They know of the Christ-followers and fear them as an unknown mystery. Scores of women and children were spared by the walls of the basilicas. But they weren't the only ones protected. Those vile senators and wicked magistrates hid behind the altars too. Of course, mere days afterward, they were back at their work as the enemies of the cross, claiming that the way of Christ was weakening the Empire!"

Augustine stood and turned away. He paced to the wall, stopping at a painting of Christ his mother had given him.

Marcellinus continued. "Their accusations are winning favor among the great houses. The tide is turning against us. The masses want someone to blame. And our enemy has not been idle, working to crucify our Lord all over again in the rubble of Rome." His voice turned desperate. "You must come!"

Augustine bowed his head. "I cannot. There is a battle to be fought here, as well. But I will fight for the church of

Christ. I will give my life to defend her." He walked to his friend and embraced him again. "Go back. Soon you will have a scroll written by my very hand. Use all your influence to spread it throughout the Empire. There is a greater city than Rome, and it stands untouched by invaders. It is the very city of God! Take heart, Marcellinus! We are its citizens forever!"

Some historians call Augustine the "Father of the West." His seminal work *City of God* shaped the thinking of the Middle Ages, which led to the greatest flourishing of art, music, and literature in history and planted the seeds of the Reformation.

Our personal holiness doesn't happen in a vacuum, but it has a very real impact on the world. When we choose God's way over our own way, it releases the transforming life of Christ into the earth. We've been invited to something greater than morality—we've been invited to experience the very power of God's life, which infuses our being and changes the world around us.

Final Brushstrokes

In this chapter, we see that the portrait of God is not complete if we do not consider His holiness. Much like a painting that will look flat and dead if it is missing certain hues and accents that bring the picture to life, if we do not recognize God's holiness, we are missing a fundamental part of His nature.

Not only is He holy, but He invites us to partake of that holiness. We see that to know Him means to be changed by Him. That change can bring temporary pain, but it always leads us to real joy, freedom, and peace.

In a culture that has skewed images of God, our personal holiness can show others what He is really like. Not a God who is mad at us or trying to stop us from having fun, but a God who loves us enough to conform us to His likeness, His holiness.

Discussion Questions

1. "Though holiness is never less than moral standards, it is always more than mere morality." When we are holy, we will be moral, but we must also be more than moral. What makes holiness distinct from "mere morality"?

2. Augustine had to make a decision to give his whole life over to God. This call to completely submit to God's way was what made him so hesitant to convert. In what ways have you experienced this fear?

3. If God is asking us to give up a certain sin, then it means He is inviting us into something much better. His prohibitions are invitations. How can we trust in God that He is trying to give us something better when He is asking us to lay something down?

4. Augustine's response to God's call to holiness changed the world. He went on, in many ways, to become the father of Western civilization. How could your obeying God, however "big" or "small," change the world around you?

Chapter 4

"THE ARMY"— GOD OF COMPASSION

William stood at the counter. His feet hurt almost as much as his heart did. Standing in front of him was what he estimated to be the most pitiful person in all of England. Her frail frame stood (some would say *drooped*) to no more than a few inches above four feet. A dirty scarf was wrapped around her wrinkled face and her hand shook as she offered him a small silver spoon.

William's trained eye immediately valued it at one pound fifty pence, and he hesitated as he reached to take it from her. He had apprenticed at the pawnshop for three years now. The money he earned here was the only thing keeping food on the table for his mother and brothers. His sharp eye, work ethic, and knack for numbers had made him the best pawn clerk in Nottinghamshire. But his soft heart for suffering people also made him the worst.

Compassion had always come naturally to him, but as his friends could attest, it had been set ablaze over the past few years. This had caused no shortage of controversy in respectable circles.

Just recently, William had marched fifty foul-smelling people out of the slums of Nottingham and right into the local Methodist church. The most memorable among the crew were a fisherman and his wife, whose Sunday-best clothing was smeared with fish guts. The congregation was shocked that these people didn't have the decency to change clothes. William knew these were the only clothes they had.

The big group had had to walk several miles to church and were a few minutes late. The sanctuary was packed except

for the two front pews, which were reserved by wealthy bene-
factors who paid for good seating but usually didn't bother to
show up. These dirty worshippers sat down on the open rows
and enjoyed the hymns and the sermon despite the whisper-
ing in the pews behind them.

After the service, William was called into the pastor's
office and confronted by a room full of appalled elders. He
learned two things that day: one, doing the right thing can
get you in trouble; and two, he wanted to do the right thing
for the rest of his life.

"Sir!" the elderly woman croaked. "How much for the
spoon?"

William snapped out of his daze and focused on her desperate face. "Ma'am, my name is William Booth, and I would
like to help you."

The Shortcut

> He left Judea and departed again for Galilee. And he
> had to pass through Samaria. (John 4:3–4)

Jesus was on His way from Judea to Galilee. Judea was in the south,
Galilee was in the north, and in between was Samaria. This was a small
region filled with descendants of Jews who had intermarried with
pagans due largely to the Assyrian conquest. Racial tension and preju-
dice created a strong barrier between the Jews and the Samaritans. So
much so that Jews would quite literally go out of their way to avoid
passing through Samaria.

But Jesus was not like that. He needed to get to Galilee, so He took the shortest and best route ... through Samaria. He didn't buy into the cultural pressure from the Jews to stay away from "those people." He walked right into the midst of them and found someone who needed to hear the gospel (the woman at the well; John 4:4–42).

Both Judea and Galilee were places of great spiritual significance to the Jews. In our own walk with God, we often feel it's taking a long time to get "from Judea to Galilee," so to speak. Could it be that it is because we aren't willing to go through Samaria? What if the best route to your growth in God is through the very place you're not willing to go? And with the people you're not willing to talk to?

> A woman from Samaria came to draw water. Jesus said to her, "Give me a drink." (For His disciples had gone away into the city to buy food.) The Samaritan woman said to him, "How is it that you, a Jew, ask for a drink from me, a woman of Samaria?" (For Jews have no dealings with Samaritans.) (John 4:7–9)

Jesus saw this woman's real value and treated her accordingly. Women in first-century Palestine were treated as second-rate humans. Not only was she a woman, but she was a Samaritan woman. And to make matters even worse, she was a Samaritan woman who had been in multiple marriages!

But Jesus saw right through all this into who she really was. Every person has a "Genesis 1:27 and John 3:16 value." Each person is made in the image of God according to Genesis 1:27 and is worth the blood of the Son of God according to John 3:16. Ultimately, the value of something is based on the price one is willing to pay for it. God was willing to give His only Son to save those who would believe in Him. Every person you come into contact with has that value on her head.

So, with this heart of love, Jesus asks the woman for a drink of water. By doing this, He sends a message that He sees her. That she is valuable to Him. And that He doesn't view her as someone unlovable or untouchable. He proves this by drinking water she has handled.

In every conversation we have with someone, we would do well to remember the person's "Genesis 1:26 and John 3:16 value." He or she was created in the image of God and is worth the blood of the Son of God! Every person on this planet is infinitely valuable to God and loved by God. Treat people accordingly.

Catherine was trembling slightly as she stood outside the tent. She was a strong woman and felt silly for being nervous, but she reminded herself that anyone would be in her position.

It was December 12, 1856, and in a nation that didn't recognize women preachers, she was about to stand before an audience and do what she had always longed to do: preach the gospel.

She heard her husband's gruff and passionate voice come from inside the tent and smiled. She loved him so deeply. They had made a pact during their courtship that if they were to get married, they would both love Christ more than each other. This had proved to be a wise commitment.

As they had both followed Christ with unbridled passion and unquestioning obedience, their love for one another had blossomed into something truly special. Not sentimental love like a frail flower or cold commitment like a gray cliff. But a beautiful oak tree, strong and elegant, dependable but ever-changing, always growing into new expressions of beauty.

They longed for the desperate masses to know that Christ could take any life and make it glorious.

She heard her husband make his closing remarks and introduce her.

Catherine stepped through the canvas door and walked toward the podium to an awkward smattering of handclaps. The crowd was clearly disappointed that the great William Booth had spoken so briefly only to be followed by a woman! She could see the questioning looks on their faces. "Is she going to *preach*?" "Maybe she is just going to give an update on the women workers in the Salvation Army?"

William smiled, gave her a reassuring nod, took her hand, and led her to the podium. He quickly sat on the front row, smiling like an excited boy. She placed her Bible down and stood up straight. Smiling, she closed her eyes, and with a pure sound hard-won through many hours alone with God, she began to pray.

As she prayed, a holy hush descended inside that tent. By the end of her prayer, not one shuffle of a foot or creak of a chair could be heard.

"Christ is all!" she proclaimed with a bold voice.

A woman in the back row broke into a muted sob. Several of the men leaned forward in their chairs with pale faces.

"If He gave His all for us, it is a small and joyful thing for us to give all to Him! Have you taken nine parts and given Him only one? Have you held on to your own life with hoarding arms and a greedy grip? When His nail-pierced hands are open and His bleeding arms are stretched out wide? Come to Jesus today! Withhold nothing from Him because He is withholding nothing from you! He—"

Before she could finish her sentence, a tall man ran to the altar and lay prostrate crying out to God. He was soon followed by women, children, and men of all ages.

She looked down at the front row to see her husband with hands outstretched to God, kneeling and weeping tears of unspeakable love.

Three Groups of Christians

When it comes to evangelism, there are three groups of people in the church. The first group likes to focus on our responsibility as believers to share our faith with others, but they often do this in such an extreme way that it leaves people feeling more guilty than inspired.

Compared to the overall size of the church, this is a relatively small group of people. Giving them the benefit of the doubt, as we should with all our brothers and sisters in Christ, they do have the right motives and the right heart. Further, what they're saying is absolutely true: we do have a responsibility to share our faith with others. But often the way they approach the argument and the spirit and tone in which they communicate are just not helpful. Guilt can never bring people into holiness. Only grace and truth can.

The second group of people, also relatively small, responds in the other extreme. They say, "Stop shaming me! In fact, we should not be 'witnessing' at all! It's just another form of bullying and pushing our viewpoint on others!" They believe a lot of damage has been done in the name of evangelism—and to some degree, they are right. They feel the sense of guilt we all feel when not sharing our faith with others, but instead of condemning themselves like the first group does, they figure out a way to change the rules. Taking it a step further, they even begin to portray evangelism as a moral evil.

Both extremes cause their own particular damage, and neither of them represents the heart of the New Testament in the life of Jesus. Christ never berated people who truly loved Him but were falling short, as the first group does. Yet He was willing to be bold about the truth and clear that there is only one way to salvation, which is something the second group is not willing to do.

But there is a third and much larger group that most of us find ourselves in from time to time. It is the group that simply forgets. We know Christ has clearly commanded us to preach the gospel and make disciples, but that conviction gets buried under the distractions of life. And every once in a while, when the gentle whisper of the Holy Spirit finds a quiet moment to remind us of this truth, we either feel shame, because of our neglect of it, or by His grace we respond in loving obedience.

So why do we neglect this very clear responsibility to share the gospel with others? I believe there are a few reasons. The first is the one I mentioned briefly before: distraction. Much has been made of the digital distractions of our time, and there are some very informative books, blogs, and essays on this. We all know we are distracted, and most of us don't need any data or research to prove it. We feel it in our bones. We have literally hundreds of things pulling at our attention, and we have more options than ever to escape into mindless consumption.

I believe God perfectly understands the time we are living in, and though He may be frustrated with our distracted hearts, He has compassion on us. He knows we are a weak and impressionable people thrust into an age where technology has far surpassed our moral capacity to handle it. "He knows our frame" (Ps. 103:14) I am so thankful for His patience with us, with me. So, if you feel burdened by the weight of a loud world, take heart, for He has overcome the world! The one who has overcome is also patient enough to wait for us to put down the phone, turn off the TV, and kneel before Him.

This brings me to the second reason we don't share our faith. I believe we neglect evangelism because we've neglected our joy in Christ. If we are finding no joy in Him, we will have no desire to share that joy with others. And lack of evangelism in our lives is a sign that we aren't enjoying Christ as deeply as we could be. If we don't really believe the good news is that good, then why would we be motivated to share it? Dive into the goodness of God, and you will find that you want others to share in that joy too!

The third reason is that we do not live with eternity in mind. We forget that we are called to cooperate with God and His redemptive plan for the earth. In His sovereign will, He has invited us to be mouthpieces for His good news. As Paul says in Romans:

> For "everyone who calls on the name of the Lord will be saved."
>
> How then will they call on him in whom they have not believed? And how are they to believe in him of whom they have never heard? And how are they to hear without someone preaching? And how are they to preach unless they are sent? (vv. 10:13–15a)

If we aren't evangelizing, it could be because we are forgetting that we are the "sent ones." That we have a very real commission by God to personally reveal Christ in the earth.

The fourth reason that causes us to neglect evangelism is the fear of man. Put another way: we find our identity and worth from people's opinion of us. The gospel can change this in our lives! As we come to know Jesus more and more and understand what He's done for us, we will realize that He loves and accepts us—and His opinion is the only one that matters.

We must be continually soaking our minds and hearts in the truth of God's love and acceptance; we are the righteousness of God in Christ (see 2 Cor. 5:21). The more we understand this truth, the less we will fear people's opinions. The gospel sets us free from this so we can actually love people.

If we say we love people but don't tell them the most important truth in the universe (the gospel), then we are not loving them in the way Christ has called us to.

Obstacles to Evangelism

An obstacle many of us face in sharing our faith is that we simply feel unqualified. We look at the great evangelists throughout church history and we can't even imagine having the gifts they had. But we must remember the parable of the talents. God is not asking you to accomplish what those great men and women accomplished. They had their own gifts and their own responsibilities to steward. But so do you! God has given you talents and abilities, and He's not judging us on the quantity or scale of our accomplishments. He is judging us on our hearts of obedience and what we have done with what He has given us.

You do not have to craft a perfect defense of the faith to witness to somebody. Do you ever find yourself believing that every nonbeliever is a vicious and intelligent atheist? That's a myth! The average nonbeliever is exactly that: average. Just like you and me! You don't need to have elaborate arguments or be a clever debater. In fact, those things might even cause us to be bad witnesses. Many can win the argument but fail to win the person. Christ has called us to truly love people, to look at them as souls to have compassion for, not as converts to be won.

The first preparation for witnessing is to ask God to give you love for other people. That is the first and greatest requirement for being an effective evangelist. If you let God teach you how to care for people, communicating the gospel will start to feel natural to you. You'll lose the pressure to win and the instinct to impress, and you'll simply love the lost like Christ loves them. So don't let your communication skills (or lack thereof) stop you from being obedient to Christ in this area! He will take your obedience and make something glorious out of it, if you will simply trust Him.

Wisdom to the Outsiders

> Walk in wisdom toward outsiders, making the best
> use of the time. (Col. 4:5)

How we treat those on the "outside" says so much about us. Whether you are into comic books, hunting, or expensive coffee, there are always insiders and outsiders. And we are always tempted to look down our noses at those who don't know what we know or like what we like.

Paul says in the verse above that Christians are to treat non-Christians in a very specific way: with wisdom.

What is wisdom? Simply put, it is knowledge lived. It is when we turn the theoretical into something real! Actually living out what we believe toward everyone we meet is the single most powerful evangelistic tool there is. Honoring the outsider. Loving the outsider. Serving the outsider. Truly caring about the outsider.

This is a profound way of living. A way of living that is only possible through Christ in us, the hope of glory. Are you walking in wisdom toward outsiders? Let's ask the Holy Spirit for help. For as we're reminded at the end of this verse, it is His power that helps us to be witnesses wherever we go.

> But you will receive power when the Holy Spirit
> has come upon you, and you will be my witnesses in
> Jerusalem and in all Judea and Samaria, and to the
> end of the earth. (Acts 1:8)

William paced the drawing room floor of their London home as Catherine sat on the sofa. Standing in front of them was a frail young woman with light red hair who spoke with the accent of the southern Irish counties.

William stopped at the window and stared out onto the lanes of Hadley Wood. "Where is she?"

"I found her on my patrol in Agar Town," the young woman said in her Irish accent. "We were doing our invitations to the soup hall when her mother came to me and took me to their ..." She paused. "Their home." Not wanting to describe their dwelling for what it really was: a one-room shack no bigger than two closets. "I'm used to the poor, sir, but I've never seen anything like this."

Catherine called the girl to sit down beside her. "Describe exactly what you saw," she said gently.

"It was horrible. The child lay there, and her face had an awful glow. It was unnatural looking! Her jaws were swollen and rigid with blood coming from wounds in her gums. She was in such pain!" She broke into a sob, and Catherine patted her back.

William turned from the window. "Thank you, child. You are a good soldier. You brought honor to our Lord by comforting this family. I will send someone to go look after them." He resumed his rapid pacing. "Those tyrants!" he said with a holy fury that echoed up the halls through the whole house. "We're going to stop them!"

The Irish girl wondered if this is what the Old Testament prophets looked like when they called down fire from heaven.

Catherine had seen William in this state before. She knew it meant they were about to enter another righteous battle. She was always glad to fight the good fight, but she couldn't help but feel a little weary this time. She also felt nervous about their new enemies.

William had known about the match factories for years, and he had given orders for the Salvation Army to help the suffering families as much as they could. But he knew he must do more.

The match factories of nineteenth-century England were awful places. Men, women, and children were crammed into warehouses with little to no ventilation. For sixteen hours a day, they would cut the wooden sticks and dip them into vats of white phosphorus, a very dangerous substance that is poisonous to the body. Many of the workers would contract what they called "phossy jaw," the painful and disfiguring sickness the young girl was suffering from. If the infected areas were not surgically treated, it could be fatal.

The worst part of it all was that it could be avoided by using the less toxic (but more expensive) red phosphorus. But the powerful matchstick bosses liked their low costs and high profits. All efforts to combat their abuses had failed, due to greed and corruption.

William walked to the front door of his home and opened it to the street. He turned to Catherine and the girl, a wild smile on his face. "Aren't you coming?"

They walked down Beech Hill Road at a feverish pace. They took turn after turn through a labyrinth of dodgy streets and run-down factories. Soot filled the air and with every step the streets got dirtier and the faces more desperate. William seemed to know exactly where he was going. They took one more turn at an old grain merchant's shop and then cut through a damp alley.

There stood a massive factory. It had been abandoned for years, and William had kept his eye on it. Out of breath and with his gaze fixed on the highest windows, he shouted, "We're going into the match business!"

Caring for the Whole Person

Jesus cared about people's hearts, but He also cared about their circumstances. We see Jesus saving people's souls and healing their physical bodies. He preached to five thousand families but also made sure they had lunch (see Matt. 14:13–21).

One of the great mistakes the church has made over the past hundred years is that we've focused on a "pure spirituality" that concentrates on truth but overlooks physical needs. This error started, as most errors do, with something true. Undeniably, the most important thing is for souls to be made right with God, that people believe in Jesus and are spiritually born again. But just because this is the most important thing doesn't mean it's the only thing. While the soul is vital, the body is also important. Jesus clearly communicated His priority to get our hearts right with Him. But as a part of that process, He showed His love by caring for physical needs.

Another way to think of it is that He is our creator—our good and loving creator. This means He knows what we need in a way we never could. And He has compassion on us when we suffer. Of course, this doesn't mean He will fix all our problems. But in His wisdom and providence, He always does the right thing toward us.

Jesus did not heal every sick person in Israel, after all. But don't miss that every sick person He prayed for was healed. This shows us two things: one, that He is wise enough to understand exactly what every person needs at every moment; and two, that He is powerful enough to act on that wisdom.

He cares not only for our inner lives but also for the minute details of our outer lives. Jesus illustrated this perfectly when He taught that the almighty God feeds the birds (see Matt. 6:25–26). And if He attends to that level of detail in His care for birds, then how must He view the lives of His crowning creation, humanity?

When talking about evangelism, we cannot overlook this point. If God cares not only for our souls but also our circumstances, how can we turn a blind eye to those who suffer and hurt? How can we say we care for their souls if we aren't also caring for their suffering?

If we follow Jesus, we will be safe from slipping into the error of preaching to the poor but not also feeding them. And we will not slip into the other error of feeding the poor but never sharing the gospel with them. We must do both.

William and Catherine Booth gave their lives in pursuit of this goal.

The Match Business

After buying the factory, the Booths started their own match-making business. They used the more expensive but safer red phosphorus, added ventilation, enforced strict safety standards, paid the workers more, and provided pristine working conditions.

William used all the influence he had to get shops around England to sell the more expensive Salvation Army matches. They called them "Lights for Darkest England" and advertised with the phrase, "Buy them to save lives!"

The matches sold so well that it finally put enough economic pressure on the match bosses to begin making humane changes. Working standards improved and thousands of the poor were protected from exploitation.

<hr />

This begs the question: What problems are we ignoring in our own communities? We may be overwhelmed by the great problems of the world. We may say, "But William Booth had the Salvation Army! He was a great man! I'm just a stay-at-home mom or an accountant." Once again, God is not looking at the scale of our accomplishments; He is looking at our simple acts of obedience.

Can you stop for the one? Can you help a family that is struggling to put food on the table? Can you cancel a streaming service and sponsor a hungry child? Can you buy groceries for a single mom? We can do something! And this brings God so much joy.

William and Catherine Booth were able to do great things because they had hearts that were willing to do one thing. Just try it and see what God can do!

One Thing You Can't Do in Heaven

I went to Jamaica on a mission trip when I was fourteen. We walked the streets of Montego Bay in teams, passing out tracts and sharing the gospel with people. It was so simple. In our modern age, this approach is frowned upon as simplistic and pushy. But it was neither. It was actually one of the most profound experiences of my life.

Something happens when you take a risk to share Christ with another person. It is humbling, it is fulfilling, and it is God-honoring.

In his book *One Thing You Can't Do in Heaven*, Mark Cahill makes a very salient observation. He points out there may be many things we won't be able to do in heaven, and he doesn't claim to know all of them, but there is one that he is quite sure about: in heaven, we will not be able to share Jesus with someone who doesn't know Him.[1] We will not be able to be a witness to a nonbeliever, because everyone in the new heaven and new earth will have already put their trust in Christ.

We have this one life here to tell others about Jesus. This one moment. And it is a vapor compared with eternity.

In Acts 1:8, quoted earlier, notice that Jesus does not just call us to be witnesses but to be *His* witnesses. We often get intimidated about sharing our faith with others. I think this fear is abated by remembering that we are not witnesses to ourselves, because that would be very scary! We are witnesses to Jesus alone.

And, of course, we so often overlook the obvious; the word *witness* here makes us think of court proceedings. In court, we are called upon simply to give an account of what we have seen and heard. That is what a witness does. No more; no less. A witness's only job is to be honest about what he has experienced. There are lawyers to do the other parts. That is where we come into the picture. "We are not theologians and attorneys at law defending Christ. He is not a defendant; He is God! We testify about Him."[2]

In other words, Jesus doesn't need lawyers—He wants witnesses. We often put pressure on ourselves to prove Jesus to people or to say the right things at the right time. But we were never called to be God's lawyers. What He needs us to be are witnesses. We are asked to tell others what has really happened in our lives through the power of Christ.

The woman at the well (see John 4) was the least likely evangelist in her city. She encountered Jesus, and her life dramatically changed. He saw through her secrets and knew her sin, and then He gave her the living water of grace. She was so overcome by Him that she ran into her village and boldly declared, "Come, see a man who told me all that I ever did. Could this be the Messiah?" (v. 29).

Our greatest zeal for sharing His love comes when we continually experience His love.

The world is waiting for an invitation to "Come see the Man who _____." All you have to do is fill in the blank! Come see the Man who ... restored my marriage! ... forgave all my sin! ... helped me forgive my abuser! ... taught me to love again! ... healed me from cancer! ... washed away my past and gave me a new life!

The first step to evangelizing is just filling in the blank. What has Jesus Christ done in your life? And, like the Samaritan woman, we simply tell everyone we can.

Also, notice that her zeal for evangelism came straight from a face-to-face encounter with Jesus. We live in a busy world, and sometimes we forget to pray, read God's Word, and worship. We "wander from the well." We stop spending time with the living Jesus ... and then wonder why we have no motivation to be His witnesses.

This witness-bearing is not only giving an accounting of what He has done in the past but is also about who He is right now! Is God real to you right now? When was the last time you talked with Him? Sat with Him? Spent time with Him?

Our greatest zeal for sharing His love comes when we continually experience His love.

Final Brushstrokes

The Salvation Army received no small amount of criticism and setbacks. At their beginning, they were hated by some of the most powerful people in the country. They were seen to be dangerously empowering the poor and working classes. But history has shown that the Booths founded an organization that has gone on to help millions of people around the globe.[3]

Today, the Salvation Army directly serves twenty-three million Americans a year through their services.[4] Everything from homes for single mothers to prison ministries, homeless shelters, feeding programs, and development work in the poorest nations on earth. I was recently in Europe and met a couple who led a Salvation Army home for Ukrainian war refugees.

William and Catherine Booth led an army of thousands (eventually, millions) in a war against human suffering and injustice.

When I look at the lives of the Booths, I can't help but be convicted by their dedication and sacrifice to the call of God. They believed the gospel really would transform lives if it was both preached and demonstrated. They did not make the mistake of preaching only, nor the other error of providing empty social services that omitted the message of the cross. They lived the true Christian life, boldly declaring the message with their words and humbly displaying the message with their lives.

Their lives help paint a portrait of a God who is not distant from people's pain. He longs for every person to be saved and come to knowledge of the truth. And if we know this God, then we must respond to His deep compassion.

May a wave of godly conviction sweep over us, calling and empowering us to live with the same sacrifice and faith that the Booths did—giving our lives to the great campaign of winning lost souls in a world desperate for the love of Christ.

Discussion Questions

1. William and Catherine Booth showed love and care to those who had been rejected by society. How can remembering the "Genesis 1:27 and John 3:16 value" of every person help us to do the same?

2. In this chapter, we learn that the neglect of evangelism can come from a few different causes: distraction, a lack of joy in Christ, not living with eternity in mind, fear of man, and feeling unqualified. Which of these challenges resonates most with you personally? And how does understanding your identity in Christ help with your fear of rejection?

3. In the lives of the Booths, we see an emphasis not just on the spiritual needs of people but also on their physical needs. How are these needs interconnected? How could you work to share the message of the gospel with others while also displaying the love of God in practical ways?

4. "Our greatest zeal for sharing His love comes when we are continually experiencing His love." How would experiencing God's love help you to share it with others?

Chapter 5

"THE HEALER"— GOD OF POWER

The hot stench of island warfare hung all around him. He walked along a road bordered by high grass and the loud buzz of tropical insects. He felt like a forgotten dot on this far-flung island. His boots plodded along with the numb obedience that only war can produce in a man, and his mind wandered back to his home in north Florida. Images of peach groves and cool summer swims in the lake passed through his mind. The thought made him feel happy and light, putting a new spring in his step.

He bounced off his back foot and unknowingly planted his front foot on a land mine.

A white flash of heat shot up his face and a concussion hit his rib cage like a battering ram. He flew back twelve feet and his body slammed to the ground. His loose teeth had been forced into the back of his throat, and blood began to pool in his mouth. The last thing he saw was an empty road stretching for miles. He was alone.

Paul awoke in a small bed in a convalescent hospital. He felt a light breeze through the open window beside him, and as his eyes cleared, he saw the unmistakable glow of a Pacific island sunset. His head was splitting, and he wandered in and out of consciousness. At one point, he saw a nurse walking toward him.

She turned and yelled to the doctor, "He's awake!"

Soon, he saw a group of nurses and doctors standing around his bed murmuring to one another. A calm, low male voice spoke to him. "Young man, when they brought you in, I thought it was a miracle that you were alive. But I never thought you would make it out of that coma. What is your name, son?"

"Paul." His voice was so weak. "My name is Paul."

The nurses broke into a giddy chatter, some hugging each other.

The doctor had a grateful smile on his face. "Welcome back, Paul. Welcome back."

The land mine had broken almost every major bone in his body. It had shattered his rib cage and knocked out most of his teeth. Shrapnel had ripped a hole in his cheek and taken large chunks of flesh off his scalp, arms, and legs. He had second- and third-degree burns scattered all over his body. Worst of all was that the shock of the explosion had given him a deep concussion. It truly was a miracle that he was alive, much less that he was awake and speaking.

Years later, Paul would wake up for work every day with genuine gratitude. He knew God had spared his life, and he strived to spend every moment with excellence and joy. He was a good dad and often spent long periods of time playing with his children even as he grimaced from the shock waves of pain that still shuddered through his body. His injuries had included major nerve damage, which caused bouts of intense pain. Still, he gratefully went to work as an engineer to provide for his family.

One day, something changed. He could feel his body finally beginning to shut down. Soon, he wasn't able to get out of bed. But he managed to get work done from home so the family wouldn't lose his income. In December of that year, he went to the doctor, desperate for some ray of hope. Instead, he was given the shattering news he had long feared: His vital organs were struggling to keep pace. He was dying. The doctors weren't even able to guarantee that he would make it to Christmas.

A few days later, a friend told him of a woman named Kathryn Kuhlman. He told him of the many miracles that had happened in her meetings in Pennsylvania. Paul believed that God could heal the sick, and now he was desperate enough to try anything. The problem was that Miss Kuhlman held meetings in Pittsburgh only, and he lived in Florida. His body was in such a state that he could barely walk from his bedroom to his front door, much less make a twenty-hour bus trip by himself. It was no exaggeration to say that the travel could very well kill him.

But his choice was a simple one: he could either stay home and die or risk death to possibly receive a miraculous healing. His family booked him a Greyhound ticket to Pittsburgh, and with tearful farewells they loaded him onto the bus and waved goodbye.

An Invitation

In 2019, a friend called me and said, "Jack, you've got to come with me to Brazil." I had actually been there a few times with the Leeland band, and it is a wonderful place. But when my friend began to describe what he had seen, I knew this was going to be a different kind of trip.

He told me he had seen blind eyes opened. People with metal in their bodies from corrective surgeries had received full range of motion restored to their arms and legs, when they could barely move them before. In some cases, the metal itself had actually disappeared, later confirmed by X-rays.

Now, my friend had grown up in the same charismatic circles as I had, and he had seen the abuses of different "healing evangelists," so he had a healthy skepticism. But his doubts had evaporated when he'd witnessed dozens of these miracles over the course of one week. The trip was with Global Awakening, Randy Clark's healing ministry.

I agreed to go with them, and in December 2019 I saw exactly what my friend had witnessed. God was undeniably healing people who were suffering from pain and sickness. Another person on the trip saw an elderly woman receive sight in an eye that had been completely blind.

I know God heals, but I needed to experience this reminder that God is way bigger than I know. And He wants to lovingly invite us all into experiences that will continue to stretch our faith.

Healing miracles were an important part of Jesus' earthly ministry. So if you, like me, believe that we are called to Christlikeness, then we must face the topic of healing.

If you have any hurt or fear about this topic, I completely understand. I myself have prayed for people who did not receive healing.

That is hard to process. But it's okay to come to God with our hurt, confusion, and doubt and still believe that His Word is true.

The Bible is very clear on this issue. I chose the story of Kathryn Kuhlman because her life is an irrefutable example that God heals today. He can even work through people who, like her, were imperfect and in need of God's grace. Because those are, in fact, the only people He *can* use.

According to Paul, the bus ride was torturous. There was no position comfortable for his body, and every bump in the road sent another shock wave of pain through his limbs. With every passing hour, he felt his struggle for survival intensify. What had begun as a painful bus trip had turned into a fight for life.

He finally made it to Pittsburgh where his cousin picked Paul up to take him to his home. But Paul was so glad to have made it alive that he asked his cousin to immediately take him to the hall for Kuhlman's evening service. His cousin helped him up the steps, and it was all he could do to stand when he made it to the door.

Then he received the crushing news that there was no service that night. He must wait two days until the next meeting, which was to be on Sunday morning.

It's hard to communicate in words the despair he felt and the overwhelming temptation to just give up. But he found strength from somewhere. He knew he had to hold on. For the next forty-eight hours, he cried out to God, asking Him to enable him to go to the service.

With the care of his family members and the grace of God, he woke up Sunday morning and made his way to the hall. As he approached the doors, he was told that the auditorium was full and he must come back for another service.

Once again, a desperate sense of panic took hold of him, and he cried out to God for help. Soon, though, someone saw him leaning on a crutch and gave Paul her seat.

As he made his way painfully down the aisle, he was overwhelmed with a sense of peace and joy. He sat down and enjoyed the beautiful singing. When Miss Kuhlman finally came to the podium, he received another blow. Before she began her sermon, she said, "Today will not be a healing service. It will be a day of repentance and of searching our hearts."

He could not believe it. He had barely survived the journey there, only to have the woman who had been his only hope slam another door in his face.

But once again he humbled his heart, lifted his eyes to God, and said, "Your will be done."

Kathryn Kuhlman lay face down alone in the dressing room of the concert hall in Pittsburgh, Pennsylvania. Every day, she felt the weight of expectations upon her. The burdens of thousands of people desperate for healing and in need of salvation.

She had come to her favorite place again: the presence of Jesus. He was always faithful to take the burden from her shoulders and remind her of the scars on His back and the nails that had been driven through His hands so she didn't have to trust in her own strength anymore. Being in His presence was both a luxury and a necessity, equally for her delight and her survival. She knew that this weight would crush her if she tried to carry it alone.

At that moment, an impression came upon her heart that tonight's meeting would be different. She felt a clear command from God that she must not emphasize healing but focus the gathering on repentance. Her heart sank at the command. What of the scores of people in there who had driven hundreds of miles for a physical healing?

She knew the answer to this without the Holy Spirit having to say a word. What good is a healthy body when you have a dying soul? What good is a miracle on the outer shell of the body without the miracle of inner transformation of the heart? She gave her loving yes to her Savior, stood up, and walked out toward the platform.

Is the Gift of Healing for Today?

Some of the most influential Christian voices in my life have been from the Reformed stream of the church, particularly the Puritans. So

I have benefited greatly from that tradition, and hopefully that comes through in this book.

However, one of the places I disagree with these denominations is their doctrine of "cessationism," the belief that the supernatural gifts are not for today. Cessationists argue that the miracle gifts (healing, prophecy, and the like) were in operation only through Jesus and the apostles as a means of legitimizing the newborn church. Once we were given the canon of Scripture, cessationists say, there was no more need for the miracle gifts.

I believe this is one of the most damaging ideas the church has ever adopted. It has caused so many to miss out on one of the things Jesus died to give them.

I don't have the space in this chapter to make a complete argument refuting cessationism. I point you to Jack Deere's superb book *Surprised by the Power of the Spirit.* Jack was a cessastionist professor at Dallas Seminary whose view completely reversed on this subject. He makes a compelling argument for the miracle gifts of the Spirit in the book. And the chapter "Were Miracles Meant to Be Temporary?" is particularly helpful.

Suffice it to say that the gift of healing is clearly still in operation today, just as I witnessed in Brazil. And this is not based on my experience alone, but on thousands of contemporary, documented cases of healing. Many of them through various healing ministries like Randy Clark's that are intentionally believing for these miracles. Though these gifts have been misused, they are still active, bringing glory to God all around the world.

My prayer is that right in our doubt, God would lovingly restore our desire to experience these gifts in our own lives. Because ultimately, it's not about the miracles themselves. It's about pointing people to Jesus to experience the salvation that is only in Him!

Before Kathryn Kuhlman could close her sermon, cries broke out in the congregation. People began weeping and repenting of their sins. Soon, it became one singular sound of grief as the congregation cried out to God for forgiveness.

Paul could feel something like a great wave swelling in his gut. As he had listened to Kathryn's sermon, he'd realized what a fool he had been. He understood now that compared with the sickness of his soul, the sickness in his body was only a small thing. He saw his selfishness and pride rearing up before him like a great beast, and he cried out to God, "Forgive me, Jesus!"

As the words left his mouth, he felt a great burden lift from his shoulders and a heaviness release from his chest. He knew he was forgiven. He knew that he was loved by the only one who mattered. Deep inside him was an assurance that he would spend the rest of his life on earth, and all of eternity, with his wonderful Savior.

The smile on his face must have looked as if it had risen from some deep glow in the core of his being, and warm tears streamed down his cheeks. The cry of mourning from the congregation had now turned into a shout of celebration and thanksgiving!

Paul sat a while longer in this electric atmosphere that felt like heaven, and then he heard a shout from the stage: "You, sir—stand up!" He looked up and saw Miss Kuhlman pointing directly at him. He hesitated. "Stand up and come down here!" she shouted with unnerving authority.

He fumbled with his crutches and slowly stood up. His seat was in the middle of the row, so he had to awkwardly stumble over people as they tried to move out of his way and help him to the aisle. No sooner had he made it to the aisle than he heard her voice boom over the speakers, "No crutches!"

A buzz rose from the crowd that was a mixture of excitement and nervous murmuring. He stood for a second on his crutches and felt that wonderful love of God surround him again. He simply dropped them and began to move his legs forward one by one.

Gasps came from the rows closest to the stage. The crowd began to stand to get a better look. Paul's walk became a run. He reached the stairs at the base of the stage and without hesitation bounded up each step like a young man. The crowd began to scream and shout.

When he reached the stage, he didn't stop running! He couldn't stop running! The man who had been dying just moments before was now jumping and praising God!

The next day, Paul helped his cousins pack the back of a borrowed pickup truck, and he drove himself back to Florida.

Two days later, he pulled up to his home, got out of the truck, and walked through the front door. His family was in the living room. For a moment, they sat stunned. The frail and dying man who had left the house just days before was now standing before them strong and full of joy. They ran to meet one another, weeping as the goodness of God filled the room.

Healing to Reach the World

In a world questioning the validity of Christianity's claims, we need more than ever the power that can confirm the message with signs and wonders. Miracles are not the main thing in Christianity, but they are a fundamental thing. In our efforts to put them in their right place, we can't make the error of giving them no place.

Without a doubt, there were excesses and abuses by the healing evangelists of the twentieth century (as there still are in the twenty-first). But what about the hundreds of thousands of people who were actually healed? What about the countless lives that were changed (and literally saved from dying) as people with diseases with no known cure were healed?

With every truth, there is the possibility of using the power of that truth to deceive, distort, or distract. But we must not abandon truth because it has the potential of danger or error.

We must do what the church has always done: simply hold fast to the foundations of the Word of God and trust the guiding of the Holy Spirit to protect us from abuses.

But the question remains: How can we engage a world whose intellectual map has no place for God? For many, particularly in the West, there is no great interest in Christianity. We now face a new generation that has constructed their own definition of meaning apart from biblical orthodoxy.

There are two courses of action to take. First, there's the logical, apologetic method. We can intellectually disassemble their bad assumptions about the world and rebuild a philosophical map in their minds that does have a place for God. That is a valid form of engaging the world and evangelizing. But there is another form of evangelism that is largely being neglected. I'm talking about a method that doesn't rely only on intellectual arguments but relies on the display of God's power, namely in physically healing bodies and revealing the secrets of men.

> **Miracles are not the main thing in Christianity, but they are a fundamental thing. In our efforts to put them in their right place, we can't make the error of giving them no place.**

This was a core evangelistic method of the early church. Paul and the other apostles clearly made use of intellectual engagement with the culture, but they did not stop there. I would argue that they did not give the intellect a preeminent place but gave first place to the power of the Holy Spirit to convince and convict the hearts of men. One of the ways the Holy Spirit does this is by breaking into someone's life and showing His goodness by healing them physically or speaking to them prophetically. Ministering to them in a way that would be impossible for a mere human. This type of evangelism is supernatural at its core.

Kathryn Kuhlman's life is a case study of someone who was overcome and almost crushed by the weight of God's compassion for the lost. This compassion led her to preach the gospel and to desire what she referred to as "the greatest miracle," the saving of a soul. But in addition to this, she staked her life on the claim that God also wanted to physically heal people as a part of His greater redemptive work.

I say she staked her life because she did exactly this. It is a deep desire in the human heart to want to be loved and approved of by others. The criticism of Kathryn's ministry and life must've been almost unbearable at times. But she once said that she could take the criticism, but what was the most painful for her was when people left the building without their miracle. She was willing to endure the suffering so that thousands upon thousands upon thousands could be spiritually saved and physically healed.

Are we willing to risk the ridicule of men so that even one can be saved? So that even one can be healed?

"What about the people who aren't healed?" is a common and understandable question. But that is my question exactly! What of the countless ones who haven't been healed because we haven't taken the risk of praying for them? What of the sick ones from whom we've turned our eyes so we don't have to answer any awkward questions? I say, let's just do what Jesus and His disciples did: let's be obedient to the command to, "Heal the sick, raise the dead, cleanse lepers, cast out demons" (Matt. 10:8a), regardless of any apparent "failures."

Praying for the sick is an act of divine love, and love never fails! So, no matter what happens, the compassionate act of believing for someone's healing is itself a success.

What if we lived this way? Thought this way? A dying world would be shocked back to a God reality that has been gone for decades. We would see millions saved! Millions coming into direct contact with the God who loves them and sent His only Son for them!

◆

The little girl knelt next to a small cot. Tears dropped from her cheeks, mixing with the dust on the dirty wooden floor.

She was nine years old but looked not a day older than seven. Her wild red hair sat messily on her lowered head. But her broken voice rose like the scent of crushed roses from that little house.

"I am nothing, God," she said. "Dear Jesus, I have nothing to offer You. Most people are born with at least one talent. I haven't found any. I've looked my whole life. I know it. Even my family knows it. I am nothing."

A faint fragrance began to fill the room and hover over the weeping child.

"Jesus, I am nothing, but I give You everything. Use me. I want the world to know how precious You are!"

How long she went on like this even she couldn't tell. But finally, she arose. There were no more tears left to cry. But as she stood up, it felt as if she had been given something. A peaceful weight pressed down on her. Some would call it a burden. But it made her feel light, like she was walking on air. It was like being surrounded by a blanket of warm air in the winter. It swirled around her, gently moving her forward and holding her tight.

She would later stand before thousands upon thousands of people and tell them about that very day. That very spot. It was where Kathryn Kuhlman died. She gave up her life and took up His.

That little poor girl from Missouri, whom no one ever really noticed, had been noticed by heaven. The girl who thought she had no gifts had just been called to carry one of the greatest healing gifts the world has ever seen.

Kathryn Kuhlman went on to see hundreds of thousands of people healed. Many healed of terminal illnesses and incurable diseases. Men, women, and children who couldn't walk would leave her meetings running. Tumors would dissolve. People blind from birth would receive their sight. A great portion of the healings happened when people had simply listened to her radio broadcast from miles away.

Her life was a showcase of what happens when someone abandons herself to Jesus and becomes a conduit of compassion for the lost and the hurting.

To her dying day, she lived for the joy of seeing the greatest miracle happen in the hearts of men: that of being born again by the power of the cross of Jesus Christ! May we live like she did. Take the risks she took. And love the way she loved.

> We are nothing, but we can give Him everything!
> "It isn't silver vessels that He's asking for. It isn't golden
> vessels that He needs. He just needs yielded vessels."[1]

How do we walk in miracles? We first have to understand that Jesus paid for them. For how could we have the gifts of the Spirit (which include healing) if Jesus had not died for our reconciliation to God? And when we are reconciled to God, we get access to the fullness of His Spirit. Fruit and gifts alike. Miracles are an undeniable part of the gospel and a way in which we can express the love of God to a hurting world.

After we understand that God wants to heal, we have to make the choice to be obedient to His command to heal the sick, raise the dead, cleanse lepers, and cast out demons. Bill Johnson said that the best way to see an increase in signs and wonders in your life is to "pray for breakthrough in private, but then take risks in public."[2]

No one lived this better than Kathryn Kuhlman. Her number-one passion and priority was knowing Jesus. Her desire to see people healed was so that others could know Jesus. And she was willing to take great risks to see people experience God's miracle-working power.

So, if you see a sick person, pray for him! We aren't praying for him to "get a notch on our belt" or have a good testimony to share. We are praying for him because Jesus gave His life to see that person saved and healed! We must keep believing and praying no matter what we see. Because Jesus is worth it all.

Final Brushstrokes

In this chapter we learned that our painting of God is incomplete if we do not acknowledge His miracle-working power. People like Kathryn Kuhlman showed the world that God is still active in healing the sick. These very real, and undeniable, accounts of miracles add a dramatic scale to our portrait of God. The Bible shows us that the Red Sea really did part, and the dead really were raised. We see a striking and active image of God, who is not detached from our world, but sovereignly intervening in its affairs.

But this picture of His power also has the dark hues of mystery. We don't understand fully how He works, but we do know that He is working. This we can be sure of. It is clearly displayed in His Word and in the lives and testimonies of millions around the world. And He is inviting us to take risks and believe that we can partner with Him in this work.

Discussion Questions

1. For some, the topic of miraculous healing is difficult. Sometimes this is because someone prayed for someone to be healed and that particular miracle didn't happen. God still invites us into faith, even with our questions and hurts. How do you feel about this topic? What are your experiences surrounding miraculous healing?

2. The story of Paul's miraculous healing is a real-life account. What part of his testimony resonated most with you?

3. In a world that is skeptical about the claims of Jesus, what do you think would happen if they personally experienced miracles in His name?

4. Kathryn Kuhlman's greatest desire was to honor God and see people believe in Jesus. She was willing to risk looking foolish to bring God glory. How could you live that way in your own world? And what risks could you take in your life in order to express God's love to others?

Chapter 6

"THE GOOD NEWS"—WHAT GOD GIVES

The room was filled with the anxious atmosphere of impending death. His brother lay in front of him, looking like a wraith of his former self. The thick layers of Scottish wool that covered him could not shield him from the cold grip of disease. He shivered violently as the family looked on with helpless pity. But somehow he managed to open his lips and let out a whisper that was not only understandable but filled with an otherworldly clarity and peace. "Read the Psalms." This spoken request filled the room with purpose and was one of those small miracles that families hold on to in such times.

Dr. Thomas Chalmers opened his Bible and began to read to his brother, his voice at first sounding too loud for the silent space: "The LORD is my shepherd; I shall not want. He maketh me to lie down in green pastures: he leadeth me beside the still waters. He restoreth my soul" (Ps. 23:1–3a KJV).

The faintest of smiles came upon his brother's face, and it seemed as if the atmosphere of the room began to warm.

I shall not want, Thomas thought. There were so many things he wanted. His restless ambition had driven him to early success. An intellectual prodigy, he'd gone to St. Andrews University at age eleven. He was not only fluent in the languages of antiquity and had a deep understanding of classical philosophy, his mind understood complex mathematical sequences with ease. People looked on in amazement at someone who seemed to have ready access to both sides of his brain; he was proficient with words and numbers, and able to understand the philosophy of the soul as well as the scientific order of the world.

Thomas's chief ambition to this point had been to gain a seat at St. Andrews as a professor. When those doors had shut in his face, he had settled for a parish pastorate. He figured that while he tried to find another pathway into academia, this would be the least demanding job to meet his needs in the meantime. He could easily rattle off a sermon on Sunday, he thought, and then be free to continue his intellectual pursuits throughout the week.

But here in this holy space, seeing his brother fade into heaven, he received an education he had never asked for. Somehow his grasp of philosophy and science felt of no use in this moment. All that mattered was whether or not it was true that, "The LORD is my shepherd; I shall not want."

He realized with an awful clarity that he was his own shepherd, and he had many wants. All his talents had seemed to make his ambition only more ravenous. A beast with an endless appetite.

He finished the reading and left his brother to his mother's care. He hoped that stepping out into the frigid wind off the North Sea would clear his mind, but today it felt like the cold breath of some awful creature. It felt like the inescapable reality of his own death, close on his heels, ready to pounce at any moment.

From Adam to Noah

I saw an artifact from ancient Sumer recently. It was a stone bull from the Mesopotamian region (close to modern-day Iraq) and dated from around 3300 to 2900 BC. Whenever I'm around antiquities, I like to pull up a biblical timeline on my phone so I can see what was happening in the Bible at the same time. I know, I'm a nerd.

For anything before 3000 BC, the Bible timeline I consulted just said, "From Adam to Noah." I looked up and there it was, a little stone bull staring at me. Now all I could see and hear was ... "From Adam to Noah." A four-word reminder of the moral history of man. In that ancient timeline we see the same kinds of sinful hearts that warp our own age.

My analytical side took over. "Who had carved this bull? Did they die in the flood? Were they closer to Adam or Noah on the timeline? Was the date wrong and was it actually made after the flood? How do they even know how old this is?"

From **Adam** *to* **Noah**

Adam, the man who was born into glory but chose sin. Noah, the man who was born into sin but chose glory. God always makes a way where there is no way.

Later that day, I heard another four words: "From Jesus to you." Jesus, the perfect One who had no sin. You, the one who has sin but can be made perfect.

That little bull reminded me how small our works are. All our striving, all our efforts to please God. "It is impossible for the blood of bulls and goats to take away sins" (Heb. 10:4). But one day, the perfect sacrifice would come.

The person who carved this bull was crying out for something, someone.

He didn't know it, but he was reaching for Jesus, the last Adam, who would make right what had gone wrong. Jesus who, like the prophet Noah, would call us to the ark of salvation. Jesus, who Himself is the ark of safety, invites us into His protection.

From Adam to Noah, we see sin and pain. But from Adam to Noah, we also see hints of the coming Savior. And from Jesus to you, we see the unfathomable love of God.

All of human history and the Old Testament were building up to His coming, this unveiling of glorious news.

The Gospel of the Age

What is the gospel? Well, before we get there, I want to start with what the gospel is not. In a culture obsessed with identity and accomplishments, people will always be desperate to prove themselves. To be accepted by a group is a deep desire of the human heart. The way our culture tells us to do this is to craft an identity and then point to our accomplishments that legitimize that identity.

For example, someone may spend many years building a persona of the successful entrepreneur. This person then has to "verify" that identity by showing signs that he is who he claims to be. So he will need the right car, the right house, and the right vacations. This vicious cycle of crafted identity and its continual requirement of proof is unending. From stay-at-home moms to accountants to pop stars to professors, everyone has an identity group they would like to be accepted by, and then they work hard to fit the description of a deserving member.

We are so terrified of being seen as impostors that this fear becomes a powerful engine of activity in our lives, driving us to do more and prove more.

Sometimes, we view God as someone in charge of just another important group we need to get into: His church. So we project an acceptable identity in order to be granted entry. Then we try to constantly show proofs that we belong as authentic members. This endless process of performance is not the gospel. In fact, it's the opposite.

◆

Thomas Chalmers sat in his study trying to prepare a sermon. This was usually an easy task for him. He could simply look at a passage and see all he needed to deliver an eloquent discourse on philosophy and morality. This time was different. His brain, usually an engine of productivity, seemed to have turned its immense energy back on itself. He could not think of one thing to preach to others.

He now saw the reality that he, not someone else, was actually the unlearned parishioner. The one who had been doing all the teaching had come to the terrible realization that he knew nothing. Or, at the very least, that he was missing some kind of keystone that would hold the bridge of his knowledge together. If only he could find it. He could feel all the information in his mind beginning to collapse upon itself, unable to bear its own weight.

He knew God was real. He knew the Bible was true. He held fast to the orthodox beliefs of the church. But it all felt dead and disconnected. Like a pile of stones with no purpose.

Dead was a word that had become all too real to him over the previous weeks. He had watched his brother slowly die before him. He had done all he could to comfort him. Usually just fulfilling his one request, to read his favorite psalms and sermons out loud.

But these passages had had a strange effect on Thomas. While they comforted his heart that there was some glorious thing he could experience, they also intensified the fear that he was not prepared for his own death. He knew that all his knowledge of the world and the church was simply not enough. The moral strength to do the things the Bible commanded was miserably lacking in his life.

He had often read, "Love not the world, neither the things that are in the world" (1 John 2:15a KJV). He felt that if there was ever anyone in the world incapable of obeying that Scripture, it was him.

His heart loved to love things. He loved books. He loved the golf links at St. Andrews. He loved the look on people's faces when he wowed them with a verbal string of pearls and the adoring murmur of the crowd as he slowly stepped down from the lectern. Something was wrong with him. Something was wrong with the whole world.

He took up his quill and managed to scrape together a sermon outline to get him through another Sunday. But how could he continue preaching when he felt so lost? He couldn't take this pain much longer. The bridge of his very life seemed to be crumbling.

The burden of "identity bearing" is crushing. The massive amount of energy it takes to project something we are not is draining. There is a better way.

In the gospel narratives, we see a surprising story. Jesus steps on the stage of history as the only one in history to have an authentic identity as the Son of God. He even provides proof to back His claim. He performs miracles that only God could accomplish. He speaks with an unassailable wisdom that leaves the smartest and shrewdest men of His time speechless.

> Imagine not having to prove yourself to anyone anymore! This is possible only by being accepted by the only one who really matters, the God who created you.

But in a radical reversal of human norms, He was not only rejected in spite of His proofs, He was rejected because of them. His very way of life was a threat to the world's system. In a world that forces people to constantly prove themselves, there is always a small group of people who get to decide who is acceptable and who is not. Jesus' life was an open rebuke to these power brokers. And He lost His life at their hands.

So, instead of being accepted, Jesus actually suffered in Himself our worst fear: the ultimate rejection. On the cross, He was shunned not only by the world but also by His Father in heaven (temporarily).

The only one who ever deserved to be accepted was rejected on our behalf.

Timothy Keller says it this way: "Christianity is the only identity that is received not achieved." In other words, in our modern culture, identity is earned, but in God's kingdom, identity is given.[1]

In the Gospels, we see Jesus actually live the identity we've always wanted: a child of God. Through His death and resurrection, He bestows this identity upon us. Not because of any striving on our part, but by simply believing upon Him and receiving His gift.

Imagine not having to prove yourself to anyone anymore! This is possible only by being accepted by the only one who really matters, the God who created you. Through receiving Jesus' identity as a child of God, we are forever accepted. And He invites us into an entirely new way of thinking and living.

◆

The summer sun beat down on the tiny, seventeenth-century parsonage. Thomas Chalmers lay in bed wracked with fever and terrified that it was now his turn to die.

The last few years had been humbling, to say the least. All his efforts to find a teaching vacancy in the college had fallen flat. He had even written a book, one that he thought would gain national attention. It was brilliant economic theory, but most of the great minds of his time paid no attention whatsoever to the book, and the experts that did notice it gave it mediocre reviews.

And here he lay. Sick with the same consumption that his brother and sister had perished from. Beside his anxiety ran a parallel track of hope. He couldn't explain it, but in these weeks of sickness, he'd felt God coming near. He couldn't shake the sense that his life had to change. All the tremors of conviction had reached their breaking point, and his heart had come to a place of decision. He knew that the choice stood before him—and the fear of physical death was nothing compared to his fear of spiritual death. What would he say if he had to stand before God this very moment?

Thomas did what he had always done in times of searching: he reached for books. First, he read the work of Blaise Pascal, the brilliant scientist who had devoted his genius to the defense of the gospel. This stirred something in Thomas. What would make a man of Pascal's talents be willing to lay down the accolades of his peers to serve God? Could God be calling him to do the same?

The next book he read was William Wilberforce's *A Practical View of Christianity*. The book spoke clearly against the moralistic Christianity of the day. Wilberforce gave a compelling invitation to believe what the Bible teaches, that you cannot earn your way into God's church but must be born again through a living faith in Jesus Christ.

With every word, Thomas felt a weight begin to lift off his shoulders. It was as if he had been carrying a boulder on his back all these years. And right there, with the sweat of fever on his brow, tears began to flow. In a moment, he saw his pride and self-reliance for the monstrous absurdities they were. He could do nothing to save himself. It was all through grace. All through Jesus.

He took his pen and wrote down these words. "The gospel is not 'do and live.' The gospel is 'believe on the Lord Jesus Christ and be saved'!"[2]

Believe, and be saved. The glorious simplicity of this invitation filled him with joy. Right there, the pastor of Kilmany trusted in Jesus Christ as his Savior.

He took the same pen and immediately began writing the first sermon he would preach when he recovered from his sickness.

Believe and Live

The gospel is not "do and live"; it is "believe and live." We want to earn everything, right to the last ounce. Whether in a Western culture of self-reliance or in Eastern cultures of shame and honor, human nature always drifts toward what we can do to control outcomes.

The curse on the outside of the garden of Eden weighs heavily on humanity, and we work by the sweat of our brow. Our tendency is to earn, always earn.

What Chalmers realized is that even with all his intellectual and moral powers, he could not produce the kind of life God wants us to have. He understood that the divine life is not the sum of our efforts, as if it were something that could be created or built by the hands of man. But it is something that has always existed and will always exist, flowing from God Himself. This life is something we are given, not something we can earn or build.

The gospel is something to be believed, not produced. The word *gospel* literally means "good news." It is a glad message informing us about something that has already happened. It can be disbelieved, scorned, or rejected, but it cannot be undone or redone. It cannot be manufactured by our efforts. It is work that has already been accomplished by the hands of God.

Christ not only experienced the rejection we are so afraid of, but He lived out the righteousness we are so incapable of. He did the work we've been fretting over. All our feverish activity to impress God is unnecessary. God invites us to simply receive what Jesus did for us.

He answers the question "Am I good enough?" by giving us His performance record. But He also answers a deeper question: "Am I alive or dead?" Only the life of God can give us spiritual life. No amount of good works can turn us from a dead person into a living person. It has to be a divine act. A miracle. "You must be born again" (John 3:7b).

And if we are at the complete mercy of this life-giver, we have to trust in Him. "Every good gift and every perfect gift is from above, coming down from the Father of lights" (James 1:17a).

How arrogant to think we could give ourselves eternal life! In a world growing more isolated and drunk on the power of technology, this temptation has new vigor. But no matter what tools are put in our hands, we will never be God. To think we can save ourselves is the ultimate affront to His glory.

"Why go all the way to India when there are souls just as lost here?" came a young, bold voice from the back of the lecture hall.

Dr. Thomas Chalmers scanned the room for the source of the disruption. The voice belonged to a divinity student who had heard about the evangelical fervor stirring in some of the students of Chalmers's philosophy class.

A little missions society had been founded by a handful of students, and this had caused quite the stir in the ancient college town of St. Andrews.

The "Scottish Oxford" had long been a place for young intellectuals to learn the great doctrines of the faith and pursue respectable careers in the church. Scotland, once the place of white-hot reformers the likes of John Knox, had over the course of two centuries fallen victim to the slow frost of man-centered religion. Chalmers himself had been a child raised in this frigid intellectualism. But there were faint cracklings of fire, and the ice was beginning to melt. This small band of young radicals was reclaiming the faith of their fathers. And one of its expressions was a new missions movement. A passionate call to take the Great Commission seriously.

"What is your name, sir?" Chalmers asked, not in the perturbed tone of a busy professor, but with the good-natured amusement of someone who was about to have some fun.

"Ian." The voice now carried the tremor of waning confidence.

"Well, Ian, being that you are a divinity student, I am assuming you have read St. Paul's Epistle to the Romans?"

"Yes, sir."

"And you believe it to be the divinely inspired Word of God?"

"Of course."

"Well, in this divine tract, we see a very sane and sober logic at work. Let's try it out. Are your parents in the church?"

"Yes, I was raised on the doctrines."

"And your grandparents?"

"Yes."

"How about your great-great-great grandparents?"

"I don't know for certain, sir. But I would venture that they held some sort of mixture of pagan and popish beliefs."

"That sounds likely," Chalmers said. "And seeing as they were bound by superstitions, who relieved them of this heavy burden and told them of the saving grace of God's elect?"

"It must have been a preacher, sir."

"That sounds likely, as well. For, 'How shall they believe in him of whom they have not heard? And how shall they hear without a preacher? And how shall they preach, except they be sent?' (Rom. 10:14b–15a KJV). St. Paul seemed to think that your great-great-great grandparents needed the gospel preached to them by a sent messenger. And if we agree with this idea in regard to Scotland, then why would this be limited by borders or a certain circumference of miles? How much more would India need this message? A land crowded with a million gods, and tens of millions of people, and not yet enough native-born preachers?"

Chalmers smiled warmly at the divinity student. "Young man, we believe that the gospel is a message that not only saves us but propels us. The gospel causes us to take Jesus' words seriously. And if He took such pains to win our wretched hearts, then ought we not take pains to tell the world of such a wonderful Savior?"

We touched on this in chapter 4, but it's worth discussing again from a different angle. Why do we find ourselves hesitant to share the gospel with others? Many Christians feel secretly ashamed about this failure. And they find themselves wishing for miraculous courage to develop in their hearts.

Many believers never share their faith at all, much less wonder whether or not they are called to be missionaries. Overall in the West, there has been a marked decrease in believers personally sharing the gospel. Why is this? There are many reasons, as we saw in chapter 4.

But here I want to talk about a fundamental problem that many in the church face, and it's this: we don't really believe the good news is good.

Those of us who have been in the church a long time know all the bullet points of the gospel:

- Jesus died in our place.
- Our sin can be forgiven if we trust in and submit to Christ as our Lord and Savior.

- Through this gift of salvation, we will spend eternity with God in heaven and begin to experience His divine life here on earth.

We can pull these facts from our brains in an absent way, like some news headline we read about an event that happened halfway around the world. We may have a real grasp of the facts, and the story may be accurately reported and beautifully written. But mere knowledge of the news is not the same as being there yourself. Being surrounded by the sights, smells, and sounds of the event is an entirely different experience. A person can read the story and recite the facts, but the one who was there in the midst of the story will be able to communicate it best. Because that person is now a part of the story.

My point is this: Why would we feel compelled to share the good news when the news hasn't become good to us?

My thesis in this book has been that Christianity is less about learning and more about remembering. For those who are already believers, if we find ourselves losing passion to tell others about Jesus, it's time for us to reacquaint ourselves with His goodness.

Because this is the reality: If you are saved, then you have been made a part of the story! You don't have to rely on dry and distant facts. The Holy Spirit can make these truths alive to you. He will remind you of all that God has done in your life. And He will lead you into more experiences and more proof that the gospel is good news after all.

One of the best indicators that we aren't finding joy in God is when we find ourselves not wanting to share the gospel with others. It's like a "check engine" light in our hearts telling us to go to God and let Him remind us of how good He really is.

Because if you think that God is mad at you all the time, why would you want to introduce other people to Him?

He loves you more than you can imagine. And that is a story worth telling.

The aged Dr. Thomas Chalmers sat by a fire in the drawing room of his St. Andrews home. He leaned on the worn armrest, and his thumb and finger tapped his chin. His eyes stared at the floor while he listened to the dialogue. More than a dozen students surrounded his chair. Some sat on the floor, some stood, and several sat crammed onto a sofa.

Books were stacked everywhere, leaning precariously in scattered towers. Some lay open with pens and journals beside them, full of a flowing cursive. This was no stuffy library for show; it was more like a workshop, and these books were tools to be used. To Chalmers, knowledge was not an end unto itself but a means to glorify God and know Him more.

The youngest member of the group was speaking. "I leave for India in the spring," he said, and the group of young men quickly grew silent and restive.

These times at Chalmers's home were always lively affairs. A chance to respectfully debate and exchange ideas among friends. But this time felt different. The young man continued in a voice they had all come to love. John Urquhart, only nineteen years old, carried an otherworldly authority and peace. His was a simple yet radical devotion to God that often left apathetic Christians feeling embarrassed. His life was a loving rebuke to the common excuses used to get out of obedience to God's commands.

"I will attend a language school in London before I leave. I look forward to preaching the gospel in a foreign language! It is news too good to be left confined to my Highlander speech."

"Teach them *real* English while you're down there!" someone on the couch said in a husky Scottish accent. The room broke into much-needed laughter.

Everyone was thinking the same thing. Foreign missions work in the early nineteenth century demanded a total commitment of one's life. Many who went to distant lands never returned to see their loved ones again, even if they were among the few to survive.

Chalmers stood from his chair, and thick silence cloaked the room. He walked to the fireplace and stared down into the low flames. "When I pastored in Glasgow, there was a young woman in my parish who lived in utter poverty. Our Bible societies did our best to help communities like hers, but it was hard work and difficult to see great changes. One Sunday after preaching, I heard a shy voice behind me."

As he spoke, the room seemed to disappear, and all the listeners were transported to the event as if they were eyewitnesses.

"Dr. Chalmers," the girl's shy voice said, "I felt something during your sermon."

"What did you feel?" I asked.

"I felt His grace." The girl smiled softly. Her face had been aged by years of crushing work, yet her countenance shone with an ageless light.

"What truth in the gospel message made you feel this today?" I asked because I wanted to understand what might get through to her community.

She seemed embarrassed but finally spoke honestly. "Well, sir, I didn't really understand what you said. I'm not as educated as you."

Now I stood embarrassed and a little rebuked. I knelt beside her. "My darling, you received an education from the only one who matters. You now know what angels long to know. God revealed the greatest mystery in the whole world to you: His love. Now go share it with everyone you know."

The fire in the library was down to a pile of orange embers. Chalmers turned to young John Urquhart as the other students leaned in closer.

"Son, you have what all the eloquence in the world cannot communicate: you know God's love. And whether here in London or in the farthest reaches of India, you must always remember that it is God Himself who turns hearts to Him. Not our sermons, not our talents. We proclaim, but He draws."

One by one, the students prayed for the young missionary until the embers of the fire grew cold.

A friend of mine, while ministering in Iraq in the mid-nineties, came across a quaint little stone church. It looked like it had been transplanted from Scotland and stood out from the rest of the buildings. Before he entered the church, he saw a plaque on the outside that listed the names of the missionaries who had planted the church. Next to their names, it said, "Sent by Thomas Chalmers."

Young John Urquhart never made it to India. He passed away unexpectedly from an illness just a few months after he had committed to go. But this young man—along with Chalmers, who mentored him—had a greater impact than either of them could have known. Chalmers's lectures, and Urquhart's holy appeals to his friends to take the Great Commission seriously, inspired several students in their class to go as missionaries to China, India, and the Middle East.

Their collective efforts over the following decades changed thousands of lives, and millions of people today benefit from the downstream effects of their work. Schools they founded educated the poorest of the poor and gave them opportunities that had been impossible before. Churches were founded that today still proclaim the gospel and bring direct relief to countless souls suffering in desperate poverty.

Chalmers's understanding of the gospel inspired a generation to give their lives so others could hear this glorious news.

The gospel is not "do and live"; it is "believe and live." When we really understand that we cannot earn salvation and that it is a gift of sheer grace, this good news transforms our lives and we will be seized by a passion for others to know.

Chalmers spent his life for this cause, and as we face a new age with all its fresh challenges, the same gospel is still the only thing that can transform a hurting world.

Final Brushstrokes

The life of Chalmers paints God in the comforting colors of gospel rest. In the same way that looking upon a beautiful piece of art can set us at ease, our image of God should have the same effect on us. The gospel takes the heavy burden of our own works off our shoulders, and gives us Jesus' righteousness instead.

Many people, when they imagine God, see Him as a hard taskmaster, angry that they can't get it together. But in God's Word, and in lives like Thomas Chalmers's, we see that His grace really is free. And the gospel really is *good* news after all. What if we lived like Chalmers in our own time, and helped the world see what God is really like?

Discussion Questions

1. In the story of Thomas Chalmers, we see the difference between intellectual knowledge and true spiritual understanding. In what ways can we guard our hearts from this error? What is the distinction between knowledge about God and actually knowing Him in Christ?

2. In this chapter, we discuss the cultural pressure to constantly project some type of acceptable identity and how exhausting that performance can be. We learn that as Christians our identity is given to us, not earned. We see that if we put our trust in Christ, God makes us His children. This is an identity that is unearned and unchangeable. In what way does that set us free from the cultural pressure to perform?

3. Chalmers discovered that the gospel is not "do and live" but "believe and live." How are those different?

4. The young men that Chalmers discipled went on to lead a massive world missions movement. In what ways can we steward our own influence and help others understand the gospel? How could that affect the world around us?

Chapter 7

"THE SONG"— GOD OF FAITHFULNESS

The sound of birdsong filled the forest. The spring sun had finally decided to shine on the village of Bridgeport, NY, and the bare tree limbs bore the faintest growth of pale green. This was Fanny's favorite time of year. The bitter days of winter were over, and the warmth of the sun's rays fell on her face. With no leaves yet on the branches, a wide expanse of sound washed around her. She could hear the high-pitched rush of the creek from half a mile away and the rustling of small animals on the brittle remains of last year's leaves. All around her, the birds continued their songs.

Fanny loved to sing. She hummed a tune in her pure, childlike soprano as she wandered through the woods. She touched the different types of branches and bushes and used them as mental markers so she wouldn't lose her way. But after what seemed like only minutes, the voice of her mother calling broke through the trees. It was time for school lessons with Grandmother.

Her feet found the little worn pathway and touched softly one in front of the other on the cool dirt of the trail.

Who needed eyesight on a day like this? Sound and smell and touch were enough.

"I'm coming, Mother!" she called as loudly as she could with a measure of sweetness in her voice to cover her annoyance. "Why can't I just live out here in April and May?" she asked the songbirds. This day was just too beautiful to be wasted on schooling. Besides, hers was a piecemeal education anyway, given by her mother and grandmother in whatever time they could spare. The village school didn't quite know what to do with a talkative blind girl.

She imagined the sound of a classroom full of laughter, and a familiar pang of loneliness stabbed her heart, an intruder into her forest sanctuary. She had reached the edge of the back field. She paused for a moment to force a smile, then ran back to the cabin.

To be alone is a painful thing. Many of us with strong, happy families often forget this, so it's not until we're in a season of isolation that we really feel it. But many around the world—due to family breakdowns, sickness, poverty, or other life circumstances—find themselves alone.

We were made for relationships, and when we're cut off from them, we experience intense pain. This is why solitary confinement has been outlawed in many countries: it's torture. God is a God of community. He is a triune God. Three in one. God has never been alone because He is self-sufficient. We are made in His image; therefore, we have a deep longing for relationship.

When sin entered the world, isolation began. Adam and Eve found out there was a boundary to paradise, and their sin put them on the outside of it. I can see them trying to look past the angel's fiery sword just to get one more glimpse of that place where they had walked with God.

From that time forward, men and women have struggled along on their own, trying their best to relate to one another, only to fumble in their attempts. In a sin-marred world, often we find friends only to lose them. Or we give love only to be hurt in return.

But God sees our pain. Jesus wept from the inside of the garden just as Adam and Eve must have wept on the outside. Who can solve a problem that sin created? Only the Holy One. He set a plan into motion.

And in Bethlehem, a baby cried.

Our forever friend had come. A Savior who would heal us of our sin to make us alive. The Spirit who would fill us and transform us. A God who would invite us back to the garden to walk with Him once again. God with us. Christ in us! "I am with you always, to the end of the age" (Matt. 28:20b).

When we say yes to this Jesus, we are never alone. In the pain of abandonment, we can run to the One who will never abandon us. We begin to see the world as He sees it. We see people as He sees them, and it changes everything! We now experience every relationship through who He is in us.

Every hurt is an opportunity to be healed and to release healing. Every attacking enemy, a target for love. Every empty room, a place to be filled with God's presence! God is with us.

And as we will see in Fanny Crosby's story, we are never alone, even amid great suffering.

◆

Fanny had collected a library in her mind. At twelve years old, her memory had already become something of legend. By now, she had memorized most of the Gospels and could recite them at will.

Her family would gather around as she quoted the Sermon on the Mount with a patient cadence. The rhythmic meter of the old King James translation lulled some to sleep. But Fanny, being the jokester she was, would shout the odd word here and there to keep her audience on their toes. Laughing from her gut, she would continue Jesus' sermon.

There was one story from the Gospels that she treasured. She would quietly whisper it in her room, running the words over and over in her mind. She imagined the sound of Jesus spitting into the dirt and what it would feel like to have the gritty mud smeared on her eyes. On more than one occasion, she opened her eyelids, expecting to see. But today was different. She just wanted to sit and listen as the scene played out in her mind.

She heard the disciples ask, "Master, who did sin, this man, or his parents, that he was born blind?" (John 9:2 KJV). This was her favorite part of the story. She waited for Jesus' response. Tears welled in her eyes as she heard His voice say, "Neither hath this man sinned, nor his parents: but that the works of God should be made manifest in him" (v. 3).

She hoped that His works could be displayed in her too, but she just didn't know how. If only she could be like her grandmother: wise, self-controlled, and humble. There was a burning desire in her that she was ashamed of—she wanted to be great. She wanted more than this little life she had.

A knock on the door startled her, and she leaped up from her knees. Someone burst into the room, and she heard the voice of her mother with the unmistakable breathlessness of joy. Fanny heard what sounded like paper flapping.

One of my great desires is to see the church become better at holding two things at once: the reality that God can and wants to physically heal people and the reality that He doesn't always heal. It's a sign of spiritual immaturity when we cling to only one or the other. Let me explain.

It is far easier to say that God doesn't heal anymore. It is also easy to say the opposite, that God always heals and that something is wrong with you if you are still sick. The truth is that both statements are wrong.

God does still heal, and we should actively pursue His healing. But God also sits with us in our suffering and promises to be our reward, even when it seems like our prayers are not being answered.

The Bible is not anti-blessing—it is full of examples of God intervening in the lives of His people. He parted the Red Sea to save the Israelites from the Egyptians. He blessed Solomon with almost unimaginable wealth. He endowed Elijah with a spiritual power that stunned the world around him. Miracles abound in the Bible. But suffering abounds too. God is not anti-blessing, but He is also not anti-suffering. The bloody record of sin stains the human story. We see pain throughout the Bible, and we see God working in the midst of it.

God clearly blesses His people ... and God clearly allows His people to suffer. Spiritual maturity demands that we admit both, no matter how hard they are to reconcile.

After all, this whole story is about God and not us. We must come to His Word and accept it as it is, not pick our preferred narrative.

For quite some time now, I've had a dream that the different streams of the church would honor one another. I wish the cessationists would understand that the gifts of the Spirit are for today. I would have them know that we can experience the spiritual gifts of prophecy and healing just as we can experience the gifts of administration or hospitality. But I also wish that my charismatic friends would understand that while God does bless and heal, He also works through suffering. I would have them know that pain is a part of the divine purpose of God and that it plays an important role in our becoming like Christ.

So, if you are a cessationist, I hope the chapter about Kathryn Kuhlman challenged you with the healing that came through her ministry. But if you are a charismatic, I would like for you to sit back and see the story of Fanny Crosby as God works through her suffering to bring countless souls to Christ even though she was never healed of her physical blindness.

God is bigger than our denominational boxes, and I believe part of what He is doing in this time is bringing us back to the truth of the Bible, even if it goes against our church traditions.

"Today, we will be introducing John Milton. His work *Paradise Lost* is possibly the most influential epic poem besides Homer's *Iliad*." The voice of the teacher filled the room. Students leaned forward in their desks. "Mrs. Claymore will be doing today's recitations. Pay attention, as there will be an exam on Friday."

The flapping paper Fanny had heard in her mother's hand was a mailed letter that changed her life. At age fourteen, she had been invited to a school for the blind in New York City. It was a new type of institution that would pave the way for excellence in education for those with disabilities.

The first week away from her family, she had wept. She had thought she'd wanted to leave home ... until she had actually gotten her wish. God had called her bluff. But soon she had made friends and settled into this new world. Other blind people surrounded her. These were friends who faced what she faced and felt what she felt.

Listening to passages from great literature was a dream come true for her. She soaked it up and placed every new story and poem she heard on the bookshelves of her exceptional mind.

Soon, her own words began to flow out of her. Back in the village, she had dabbled in poetry and become the local bard. Her poem about the dishonest miller who mixed cornmeal into his bags of flour was a favorite. But here, her writing truly came alive.

The girls would come to her room late at night and sit amazed as she would compose a poem on the spot and recite it without pause.

It wasn't long before she became the poster child for the school. The headmaster had her write poems for the dignitaries who visited. Even Secretary of State Henry Clay had listened as she performed a patriotic poem she had written fifteen minutes before his arrival.

Fanny found her voice here. But she couldn't shake the unnerving silence of God's voice.

"I am going to heaven," her grandmother had said to her as she lay on her deathbed. "Will you meet me there?"

"I hope God will help me meet you there," Fanny had told her truthfully.

She still vaguely hoped that she would go to heaven and that the works of Jesus could be displayed in her life as they had been in the man born blind. But hope was all she had, and the next steps to God were as dark to her as the blackness that engulfed her eyes. So she began to compose another poem to fill the uncomfortable silence.

Suffering is relative. There is the dangerous and acute suffering of hunger and homelessness. To not have food and shelter, the most basic human needs, is a terrible reality that most of us in developed nations never experience. Yet hundreds of millions of people across the world do.

The spectrum of suffering runs all the way from the unimaginable pain of losing a child to the more common reality of losing a job. One of the few things we can count on in this world is pain.

And it seems that some go through more of it than others. Why? This conundrum, the problem of pain, has been written about by far greater minds than mine, so I encourage you to seek them out. But the question I would like to ponder in this chapter is not a matter of *why* but of *what*.

We often get so focused on why God allows suffering that we miss what God can do through it.

So much of what we experience in suffering, whether good or bad, depends on our response to it. How many people respond to tragedy with despair and bitterness? Countless lives have been destroyed not by the suffering itself but by the response to it. Others experience deep pain yet still see opportunities to find joy. Fanny Crosby is a shining example of this.

The change of perspective from *Why is God allowing this?* to *What is God doing in the midst of this?* is a profound shift that we must make in order to live as God calls us to.

Almost every great man or woman of God I know has gone through some type of "hell" in life. Though God did not *send* the tragedy, He sent His life-changing power right in the middle of it. A power that transformed the person to become more like Christ.

Does God's power express itself in supernatural healing and provision? Yes. But that same power is also present in the darkest places and under the most terrible circumstances. The goal, after all, is to make us like Jesus. Everything we face, whether blessing or suffering, is an opportunity to get closer to that goal.

She wanted so badly to feel what this preacher was saying, but she couldn't.

People were running to the altar seemingly over-whelmed by the message of the gospel. Fanny understood what was being said, but shouldn't it move her? Shouldn't a decision this big register on the scales of her heart? *I hope there is nothing wrong with me*, she thought, not daring to utter it out loud.

The message had been clear that night. "Give your life to Jesus!" the preacher had proclaimed. "Make Him Lord of your life! Believe in Him, and you will be saved!" She had heard all this before. She wanted to respond, but with every failed attempt she grew more anxious and confused.

Why isn't this easier for me, God? The thought erupted from her heart more like an accusation than a question. Didn't He know how hard her life had been, and how she had borne it all with a smile? She knew the Bible inside and out. Her grandmother had taught her so much about Jesus. So why was this wall in the way? Why was He hiding from her?

Whether it was stubborn determination or genuine faith that moved her, she realized that she had stood in front of everyone and had begun walking down to the altar.

Her friends who had been praying for her followed excit-edly. Soon there were deacons, elders, and strangers alike crowding in on her, praying. They were there for what seemed like hours.

God had felt so far away, but the more she heard these people cry for her, the nearer He felt. It was almost as if there were an unseen war going on for her soul, and all she could do was kneel there in the vortex of intercession around her.

Then the church began to sing. It was a God poem put to music.

She knew this Isaac Watts hymn well, but something began to stir in her with each new stanza. She had loved words and poems her whole life, but these felt different. They were coming alive, feeling less like ideas and more like live embers of fire burning her heart. The last verse rang out from the congregation with pure passion:

But drops of grief can ne'er repay
The debt of love I owe;
Here, Lord, I give myself away;
'Tis all that I can do.[1]

The tears began to flow. In that moment, a miracle happened inside her. She saw with plain clarity the state of her heart. She had been holding on to her life. She had tried to keep one foot in the world and one foot in God's kingdom, but she now realized this was impossible. It was all or nothing.

Fanny felt love wash over her, inviting her to give herself away. She knew deep down that everything would be okay if she did. That she could trust this person who was asking for everything. She had memorized His words, but now it was her turn to speak.

"Yes, Lord. I surrender myself to You."

She held the baby in her arms. The sound of his little voice had filled their apartment with so much joy over the past few days. But now the silence was nearly unbearable.

During the pregnancy, Fanny had dreamed of who this baby would one day become. What conversations would they have? How many grandchildren would he give her? Would he get his father's gift for playing musical instruments or her gift with words? Maybe both!

All the moments that they could have shared together pressed down on her chest with a suffocating weight. She had not told anyone this, but one of her greatest hopes for parenthood was to get to see the world through the eyes of her own child. She imagined taking him to the zoo and asking for his description of an elephant. To have the joy of taking part in the childhood eyesight she never had, all with the unselfish love of a mother delighting in her son.

But here was a story she had not anticipated. The child had not survived his early infancy, and Fanny knew she had a choice to make in this moment.

The suffering of her blindness had taught her how to find joy and contentment in her limitations. More than that, she considered her blindness an advantage and could now trace God's providential hand working through all the challenges she had faced. Her life was truly a witness to those around her. But this was a new kind of pain.

The thought came to her mind that she didn't deserve this. She had been through so much and had still given her life to Jesus. Couldn't He give her this one thing? But as soon as the thought came, her well-trained heart knew what to do with it. She took her confusion and laid it as an offering at the feet of Jesus.

"I told You that everything I have is Yours, and I meant it. You gave me this beautiful child to carry, but now You are carrying him in Your arms. You are his parent now, and why would I begrudge this child the glorious gift of being in Your presence? His eyes are seeing something far better than the things of this world. He is gazing on Your face."

As waves of grief continued to come, she sat down and began to pour out her heart through a pen. Moments later, she had written lyrics to a new hymn, "Safe in the Arms of Jesus."

It would go on to become one of her most popular hymns and a comfort to countless people around the world who had lost loved ones. It was even played at the funeral of President Ulysses S. Grant on August 8, 1885.

Every good thing you have experienced was God trying to show you what He is like. The smell of a campfire on a crisp, autumn evening. The belly laugh of a toddler. The taste of Mom's chocolate pie. A glass of ice-cold water after mowing the lawn on a hot summer day.

All these things are small graces pointing to the author of grace. In the chapter on joy, we talked about C. S. Lewis's idea that all joys are signposts. Where we get stuck is when we stop and camp out by the signpost instead of moving on to where it is pointing.

God wants to bless you. In the Old Testament, one of God's names is Jehovah Jireh, which means "*God is a provider.*" But every blessing He gives, whether big or small, is a signpost pointing you down the road to Himself. He is trying to use these good things to reveal Himself as the true source of goodness. And so often, we stumble over these blessings and begin to worship the gifts rather than the giver.

But if blessing reveals God's nature (His goodness), then suffering is an opportunity to be conformed into that nature. Blessing reminds but suffering transforms. The goal of both is to draw us closer to God.

People who go to the gym and lift weights are familiar with the concept that pain brings transformation. This is a principle built into the very nature of things.

It is no different in life with God. We must be mature enough to hold these two things at once: God does want to bless us in order to reveal His goodness, but God also works through suffering to conform us into that goodness.

Olives and grapes are wonderful in and of themselves. But we get to enjoy oil and wine only by crushing them. If we will give our lives over fully to Jesus and trust Him in suffering, the painful pressing will diffuse His life and joy to all around us.

This is the promise of the gospel: no matter what we experience, whether blessing or hardship, it offers the opportunity to know His goodness and display Him to a hurting world.

The music from the piano echoed off the high, paneled walls of the sitting room. The grand windows looked over the lawn of a vast estate on the outskirts of the city.

Mrs. Phoebe Knapp was playing the piano today because the organ was being serviced. The wife of Joseph Fairchild Knapp, founder of Metropolitan Life Insurance Company, Phoebe was a budding music composer and supporter of the arts, hosting banquets and artistic showcases at their manor home.

Phoebe attended the same church as Fanny and had become a close friend and occasional musical collaborator. Today, Fanny sat on a chair next to the piano bench, with her head bowed.

The number of hymns Fanny had written since her conversion was truly astonishing. She knew that giving her life to Jesus meant giving Him her talents too, and she wanted to write songs that would tell the story of the gospel. If they were instrumental in saving even one person, then all her hard work would be worth it.

It hadn't taken long for Fanny's name to become famous. Just a few years into full-time writing, her hymns had caught fire in the church in America and eventually around the globe. The great evangelist Dwight L. Moody used her songs in his meetings to great effect, and many souls were coming to Christ.

She was so prolific, in fact, that hymnbook publishers asked her to begin writing under different pen names so that *Fanny Crosby* wouldn't be the only name in the entire catalog.

She had many wealthy and influential admirers, Mrs. Knapp being one of them. They had offered her gifts and money, but Fanny had refused. She was paid a small amount for each hymn she wrote, and the royalties for global sales went directly to the publishers. She lived simply, choosing to be among the poor in the notorious tenement housing of nineteenth-century New York City. She wanted to be close to the various missions she loved, and she spent hours sitting with the broken young men who came to the newly established YMCA for care.

"What do you think of the tune?" Phoebe asked nervously.

People were always asking Fanny to write lyrics for their melodies, but she didn't mind. It was a joy to serve others with her gift. Fanny lifted her head, and a radiant smile from some place of deep contentment lit her face. With the excitement of a child, she said, "The melody is saying, 'Blessed assurance, Jesus is mine!'"

Suffering and the Mission of God

There is a lot of strategizing happening in our day about how to reach a "post-Christian" culture. It is a subject well worth our time as we consider the days ahead.

How do we preach the gospel to people who don't feel guilt because they don't believe in sin? People in the world have feelings of pain and confusion, certainly, but this new generation does not have the inherited religious values the previous generations had. Every influential voice in education, media, and psychology has told them to do what makes them happy. So how do we reach a group like that? We are going to have to find new and creative ways, and suffering can teach us here.

> **Pain is an opportunity to glorify God in a world that doesn't know how to handle suffering.**

The one great common experience throughout all human ages has been pain. No amount of technological advancement or time-saving conveniences will be able to exempt us from it.

The singer/songwriter J Lind says it well in his song "Letter to the Editor":

> *Soon all the cars will drive themselves.*
> *Some people think that will really help ...*
> *help me complain about something else.*[2]

Until Jesus comes back and makes a new heaven and a new earth, every human will suffer in some way because of the effects of sin.

As Christians, we have an amazing opportunity to witness to this world by how we handle our own suffering. The world has only four answers for pain: run from it, medicate it with the opiate of sin, stoically deal with it, or blame someone else for it. The believer has a radically different response. Shockingly, and against all our instincts, we are told to rejoice in it!

> Not only that, but we rejoice in our sufferings, knowing that suffering produces endurance, and endurance produces character, and character produces hope, and hope does not put us to shame, because God's love has been poured into our hearts through the Holy Spirit who has been given to us. (Rom. 5:3–5)

As I said before, the Christian must see suffering as an opportunity to know God and become more like Him. If that is the case, then pain is actually a unique opportunity for us. What greater gift is there than to experience the one true God and be more like Christ? This is why we are alive!

So, while waiting for that miracle or believing for God to change a certain situation (and we should never stop believing for those things), we still rejoice in Him. We don't rejoice because of the suffering, but we do rejoice in the suffering. Because Jesus is with us.

If our culture saw believers live this way, they would have no other explanation but to admit that they see God's power at work in us.

Pain is an opportunity to glorify God in a world that doesn't know how to handle suffering.

A frail but energetic elderly woman stepped off the trolley car. Wearing the shades that the blind people of her day typically used so others would be aware of their disability, she walked amid the bustling crowds of New York City.

Since the woman was now in her eighties, her family had all but begged her to move back to Bridgeport to get out of the city. She had begun to struggle with her health, and living in the dirty and increasingly dangerous metropolis simply wasn't wise for her anymore.

She had agreed to move back to the country, but only on the condition that she could still take her regular speaking engagements and continue to minister to the poor.

However, she sensed that something had changed in the city. The people were less accommodating and patient. In earlier years, she could always find plenty of people to help her, but she sensed now that she was just another person in a cacophony of distracted voices. No one paid any attention to her.

She finally found her way to the meeting hall where she was expected as a guest speaker.

When the door opened, she immediately knew the room was full by the warm and humid smell that can come only from densely packed people. She touched her right hand on the end of a wooden pew bench and began to walk down the center aisle. The loud chatter of voices gradually settled into a quiet attentiveness by the time she reached the front row.

The director of the Brooklyn youth mission guided her to a bench. "Welcome, Mrs. Crosby. You can take a seat right here. Are you ready to speak after I give a brief introduction?"

Fanny smiled and nodded as she sat down to rest her sore feet for a moment.

The director took the podium. "Thank you all for coming to this special assembly. Our guest needs no introduction, but for the few here who may not know her, I will give a brief description. Fanny Crosby is the most prolific hymn writer in the history of our nation, and possibly in history of the Christian church.

"While just a baby, she lost her sight when doctors applied hot poultices to her eyes as a remedy for sickness. In spite of her challenges, she has faithfully served the Lord and been a friend to home missions her entire adult life. Many people in this crowd have been beneficiaries of her kindness and brilliance. We are honored to have this giant of the faith here with us today. Would you please welcome Mrs. Crosby?"

Fanny took the podium as the crowd cheered loudly. When the noise dissipated, her small but strong voice cut through the silence.

"My young friend gave such a wonderful introduction, but I must kindly correct him on one point. He said that my life's work for the Lord has been *in spite* of my blindness. And although I understand what he means, I would say the exact opposite. I believe that every hymn I've ever written, and every good thing I have ever done, was not in spite of my disability but a direct result of it.

"God has shown me His goodness through my blindness. I am actually a little embarrassed by the compliments I receive, because I know my own heart. I believe that blindness saved me from worldly distractions that could have destroyed me. Or at the very least rendered me incapable of giving my all to God. I would never have written this many hymns without the advantage of blindness and the opportunity to have my ears and mind focused on His voice.

"This brings up my question for you today. Many young people in this room have challenges too. You may not be blind, but everyone has some suffering to bear. Moses had difficulty speaking. Abraham, though he was the 'Father of the faith,' was sometimes cowardly to the point of lying. David's lusts almost destroyed him. And Peter's wild emotions seemed too much for anyone to control. But God uses our weakness to show His strength. And if you will let Him, He can do the same through you. It doesn't matter if you are poor, uneducated, addicted, or afraid. He died for you and is alive to save you. I pray that you would trust in Him today. Not in your own strength or ability, but in His power to make your life something beautiful."

She heard a low murmur of voices in the audience. She sensed that the crowd had noticed something. The director whispered that a young girl in the back row had raised her hand. "What is it?" Fanny asked with a smile. No answer came. "It's okay. You can speak up."

The nervous voice of a young girl came from the back of the room. "Mrs. Crosby, don't you wish you could have seen the faces of the people you love?"

Embarrassed adults began to shush her.

"It's all right!" Fanny said. "It is a good question. One I have thought about often." She smiled and turned her head in the direction of the little girl. "My darling, I will see the faces of those I love one day. But before I see their faces, I will see my Savior. I have a privilege that those with sight don't have. My eyes have been reserved for Him alone, and when they finally open, His will be the first face I see."

Final Brushstrokes

In the life of Fanny Crosby we see that it is possible to hold on to God's faithfulness throughout suffering. From her story, our portrait of God takes on the solid and dependable hues of hope. Like the sun invariably rising, no matter how dark the night may be, the glimmer of God's goodness is on its way. Our job is to expect that grace, and faithfully wait for Him during our pain. Fanny Crosby shows us that God will not only work to end our suffering (as He certainly does) but will also work through our suffering to accomplish truly amazing things. Every good thing that happens to us is meant to remind us of what God is like, and every bad thing that happens to us is an opportunity to be formed into that divine goodness. Either way, we are the recipients of grace.

Discussion Questions

1. In this chapter, the author explores the ideas that God does bless and miraculously intervene in His people's lives but that He also works in the midst of great suffering. In what ways can we celebrate both of these truths? Which one do you have most difficulty with, and why?

2. Blessing reveals God's nature (His goodness), and suffering is an opportunity to be conformed into His nature. What good thing reminds you of God's goodness? And what painful things have helped form you into a more Christlike person?

3. Pain is an opportunity to glorify God in a world that doesn't know what to do with suffering. How could your response to suffering serve as a witness to the faithfulness of God?

4. Fanny Crosby chose to consider her blindness a blessing and actually said that it contributed to her prolific songwriting. Is there a challenge in your life that you could view with a better perspective?

Chapter 8

"THE CREED"— GOD OF TRUTH

The city of Alexandria sat glittering like a pearl on the coast of the Mediterranean. The Pharos island reached north into the ocean like a curved finger, connected to the mainland by a man-made stone pier. On either side of it lay harbors with calm, emerald waters filled with sails and ship masts of all sizes. On some days, it seemed that you could walk across the entire width of the harbor, deck by deck, without touching a drop of water.

Alexandria had become one of the most important trading centers in the world, and great cities like Rome and Constantinople had become dependent upon the grain exports from this ancient waterfront.

The famous Pharos lighthouse stood tall on the island, dating back to the time when the Greeks ruled the known world. It had guided countless ships and wanderers looking for fortune, safe passage, and knowledge.

In Alexandria, intellectual and commercial life flourished alongside one another. In past centuries, many people had come to seek answers in its vast library, which had contained the largest single collection of written works on the planet before its destruction by a fire in AD 31. Despite this tragic loss, the city's vibrant culture of scholarship and philosophical rigor had survived.

Jews, Egyptians, Greeks, and immigrants from distant nations mingled together in a place that had come to pride itself on its peaceful diversity.

It was from this place that a fierce debate over the nature of God Himself would spread through the Roman Empire and have far-reaching implications for centuries to come.

"I baptize you in the name of the Father, the Son, and the Holy Spirit," said the young man, his fingers holding his friend's nose as he plunged him into the brown waters of the Nile.

The other boys cheered from the riverbank as their friend emerged.

The youth leading the ceremony, no older than sixteen, raised his hand to hush them. "I appreciate your excitement for our brother. But please don't draw any unneeded attention. I don't have permission to do this officially yet."

"Don't worry," the boy who had just been baptized said. "You have to practice on someone, so it might as well be us. Well, everyone except Lucius. He's still learning to swim."

More laughter from the riverbank.

"And you need to work on your dunking," the baptized boy said with a playful punch on the shoulder. "It was a little heavy-handed."

The aspiring priest shook his head and smiled as he led his friend out of the water.

"Do you know why I've brought you here?" asked an elderly man dressed in the crimson robes of a bishop.

"No, Your Holiness." The young man before the bishop was small for his age, with the dark skin of the local Egyptians. His eyes had a sort of fire in them that had troubled some of the authority figures in his life. He carried a restless energy that some saw as rebellion and others saw as passion. But it seemed evident to all that he was destined for something grand in scale, and his future, whether for good or ill, was still hanging in the balance.

The bishop's commanding voice broke the silence. "I was near the river last week. And I saw you baptizing your friends."

The young man froze. How had he been so foolish? He kicked himself for not choosing a more secluded spot. Shame and its attendant, anger, welled up in his heart.

"Have your friends professed true faith," the bishop asked, "or were they just mocking?"

"They have told me they truly believe. And we did not mean to be disrespectful, sir. I have thought of being a priest one day," the young man said, not sure what trap he was being led into. "And I ... I was practicing."

The bishop stepped to within a few feet of the young man, whose head instinctively dropped as his elder approached. The bishop looked down on him with a face of grave importance. "I brought you here today to tell you that I am approving their baptism into the faith and confirming their acceptance into the church."

The boy's head shot up, mouth open, with the vacant look that only true shock can give.

The bishop let out a hearty laugh, clapping his heavy hands together and smiling with a fatherly affection. "I heard every word you said. You led the baptismal rite to perfection. You should give our priests a course to refresh their memories."

"But I was just practicing."

The bishop put his hand on the young man's shoulder and led him to a window across the room that overlooked the old city and harbor of Alexandria. "My son, do you see all those people? Merchants and beggars, soldiers and criminals alike? We can only see what they are doing. We cannot see what they are thinking. Only God can peer into the hearts of men and know their true desires."

He regarded the youth beside him. "Last week I saw a young man boldly professing the truth and leading his friends toward it. Whatever your intentions were, that is between you and God. And He is the One who will convict and correct your heart. But the truth is the truth, no matter what our motives are. And that which is false is false, no matter how good our intentions. Now, go home. Help your parents with the chores. We will talk more about this soon."

The boy, not quite sure of what to say, simply nodded and turned to leave.

"Athanasius," the bishop called as the boy was crossing the threshold. "When God gives you the gift to lead others, you must choose carefully where you go because people will follow. And if you are ever unsure of where to turn, look for the truth and simply walk in its direction, no matter the obstacles that stand in the way."

The truth exists, and it is possible to know it. One of the things God communicated through the incarnation (the act of God becoming man) was that the truth actually can be known. Known in the same way you can know what color your mother's eyes are or how many fingers you have!

Jesus, who was fully man and fully God, said that He was "the way, and the *truth*, and the life" (John 14:6). So, first and foremost, when we talk about truth, we are actually talking about a person. Jesus, the truth Himself, became someone who could be touched, who had a certain type of hair and whose nose and ears and fingers had distinctive peculiarities. Truth came close. God was showing us that He *wants* to be known and that He *can* be known.

So, if we are able to know the One who is truth and from whom all reality proceeds, then we can also know what is true in every other area of life.

The sun rises in the east. Water freezes at thirty-two degrees Fahrenheit. God made a world with clarity and order, and though life may seem mysterious, the answers will come for those who seek them. From Isaac Newton to Albert Einstein, you see this principle at work. We live in an ordered universe, and though its complexities often baffle our minds, that doesn't mean answers cannot be found.

We live in a contentious age where confusion abounds. It is a time when almost everything is politicized, and each side says that the other is spewing disinformation. So what do we do in a world where it seems like we can't really know the truth?

Well, as we said above, we first have to know the truth does actually exist. Yes, we each have our own lived experiences, but that is not the same as each having our own truths. There is one objective reality, and God in His goodness and mercy will show us that reality if we seek it.

Secondly, we have to know how to resist the lies. What is heresy, after all, and how do we protect our hearts against the attractive qualities of untruth?

Lastly, we need to understand the way in which God has called us to seek after the truth and to fight for it. Athanasius is a great example of someone who tried to live in this tension. He saw clearly something that was simply true about God, and he devoted his life, at great cost to himself, to defend that truth and live for it. But he was still a human and made mistakes like the rest of us. This reminds us that, in our zeal, we must remember the *way* in which we defend the truth is just as important as *what* we are defending.

The chapel filled with the expectant hum of those who had been unexpectedly caught up into great events. The thick Byzantine walls allowed only a few small windows, and the light of hanging lamps cast their warm glow onto the domed ceiling. Painted icons of the apostles gazed down on the room full of bishops, deacons, and theologians from around the Empire.

There were 318 of them in all. The same number, in fact, of the company that had risen with Abraham to fight their enemies and rescue his captured family (Gen. 14:14). A fitting metaphor for those in this room who had traveled far to fight the great enemy himself, Satan, whose ancient deception was working to tear apart the family of God again.

Athanasius, now twenty-seven, sat on a low bench near the front of the proceedings. On the row in front of him was the man who had become like a father to him. Alexander, the great Bishop of Alexandria, had taken him under his charge when he was just a boy and trained him in the ministry. Now a deacon in the church and the most trusted advisor to the bishop at this council, Athanasius felt the weight of honor and anxiety all at once.

Just a few feet away was the most powerful man in the world. Emperor Constantine had summoned them all to his lakeside summer retreat in Nicaea to resolve the arguments that were plaguing the church. His faith, though seemingly genuine, was still growing, and the political strain caused by this theological rift between two opposing factions in the church was too great a threat to the Empire for him to dismiss. Christianity, he knew, would either be a deep foundation holding up the structure of society or an earthquake tearing it down. This chapel on his estate was now the fault line where two great forces met.

Arius led one of the forces. Arius was an intelligent and popular leader who had proven himself a capable pastor and wise theologian. He cared deeply about the dignity of the eternal God and had been wrestling with a problem that had haunted him for most of his adult life: How could Jesus be both fully man and fully God?

If God were to become a human, He would have to somehow limit Himself—the One who by definition is without limits. And if Jesus were "begotten," then that must certainly mean that He was, in a sense, *created*. If Jesus had some sort of beginning, how could He be God in the same sense as the eternal Father? In order to protect the integrity of the uncreated and transcendent God, Arius believed that Jesus had to be in some sense secondary and inferior.

He had been teaching this doctrine for years, and the belief in Jesus' secondary nature had spread like wildfire in the church. To help the people remember the core of his teaching, Arius had even created a simple jingle: "There was a time when He was not."

This was no small debate. Indeed, the very claims of the gospel were at stake. Arius taught that the church could survive just fine by defining Christ as something like a demigod, far higher than the angels but certainly less than the one eternal Father.

Athanasius squirmed in his seat as Arius spoke before the emperor. His mentor's words rang in his mind: *That which is wrong is wrong, no matter what the intentions are.* And though both sides were trying to find the truth, only one of them could be right. There was no way to come to some sort of compromise here. Jesus was either fully God or He wasn't. In that sense, at least, the debate was very simple. Simple as it was to define, though, Athanasius would spend his life in this fight.

Despite Arius's compelling oratory, the Council of Nicaea sided with Athanasius. It condemned the Arian concept of the trinity and its definition of Christ as something less than fully God. To help them articulate their view, the council used the Greek word *hormusia*, which means *"of the same substance,"*[1] when speaking of the three persons of the Godhead. Under the supervision and approval of the emperor, the bishops crafted a creedal statement that affirmed the divinity of Christ. The Nicene Creed has been the basis for biblical, orthodox theology throughout the centuries.

We believe in one God,
the Father, the Almighty,
maker of heaven and earth,
of all that is, seen and unseen.

We believe in one Lord, Jesus Christ,
the only Son of God,
eternally begotten of the Father, God from God,
Light from Light,
true God from true God,
begotten, not made,

of one being with the Father;

through him all things were made.

For us and for our salvation

he came down from heaven:

was incarnate of the Holy Spirit and the Virgin

     Mary,

and became truly human.

For our sake he was crucified under Pontius Pilate;

he suffered death and was buried.

On the third day he rose again

in accordance with the Scriptures;

he ascended into heaven

and is seated at the right hand of the Father.

He will come again in glory to judge the living and

     the dead,

and his kingdom will have no end.

We believe in the Holy Spirit,

the Lord, the giver of life,

who proceeds from the Father [and the Son],

who with the Father and the Son is worshiped and

     glorified,

who has spoken through the prophets.

We believe in one holy catholic and apostolic Church.

We acknowledge one baptism for the forgiveness of

     sins.

We look for the resurrection of the dead,

and the life of the world to come. Amen.[2]

Athanasius sat at his writing table as the imperial troops approached the city. He remembered the conversation he had had as a boy with Bishop Alexander in this very room. Now a bishop himself, over the years he had found an even deeper respect for his spiritual father. The weight of leadership was tremendous. His roles as a local pastor, shepherd of the people of Alexandria, and regional overseer for the churches of Egypt were all-consuming.

Yet the fires of theological debate were still raging. Arius had died suddenly years before, but his ideas had survived. So Athanasius wrote feverishly to defend the Nicene Creed against the dogged influence of Arianism. Though Arius had been a man who genuinely sought the truth and had the best intentions, wrong ideas have consequences ... and old heresies find new friends. Arianism had been accepted by ambitious and truly wicked men both in the church and in the government.

One of those men was marching on the city at the head of imperial troops, ready to become the new bishop of Alexandria.

Athanasius knew that these could very well be his last moments in this room. He had already experienced one exile and knew that another one was upon him. The political tides had shifted. Constantine was dead, and Athanasius had fallen out of favor with the new regime.

Anger began to well in his heart, and it brimmed over into tears.

A young deacon burst through the door laboring to catch his breath as if he had just run a long distance. "Father, they have taken the harbor. You must leave now."

Athanasius closed his eyes and set his heart on God. "Jesus, Your honor is worth a lifetime of dishonors. The truth of who You are is worth the lies they have spoken about me. If I have You, I have everything. If I lose You, I have already lost all."

His young priests arrived and ushered him toward concealment. His head spun as he was swept down a stone staircase and into the back courtyard of the church. He heard the shouts of people in the streets and the sound of shattering glass. Smoke rose from burning ships in the harbor.

The priests took Athanasius to the door of a small home where a man welcomed him in. Without a word, the man led Athanasius to a small, damp cellar, ushered him inside, and shut a wooden trapdoor above him. The man quickly pulled a dusty rug over the door, plunging the small space into darkness.

◈

All heresies are a response either to something God said that we don't agree with or to something God commanded that we don't want to obey.

The conscience that God gave us is a powerful thing, and we don't like to suffer under the pressure of guilt. So we create spiritual explanations for our disobedience, and we redefine the truth and the law to fit our desires. If we can change those things in our minds, then we feel a great moral and psychological relief.

We are all susceptible to this, so how do we keep from doing it? It's a one-word answer: humility.

Andrew Murray defines this often-misunderstood idea in his book *Humility* as "the place of entire dependence on God." He says humility is "the highest virtue of every creature and the root of every virtue. And so pride, or the loss of this humility, is the root of every sin and evil."[3]

All heresies are rebellion against God. And all rebellion against God starts with pride. Therefore, the remedy against heresy is humility.

How do we cultivate true humility? Isn't it impossible for humans, who are notoriously self-centered? Well, it is possible, after all.

Humility comes from seeing God. Isaiah 6 clearly illustrates this.

> I saw the Lord sitting upon a throne, high and lifted up; and the train of his robe filled the temple. ... "Woe is me! For I am lost; for I am a man of unclean lips, and I dwell in the midst of a people of unclean lips; for my eyes have seen the King, the LORD of hosts!" (vv. 1, 5)

When we see God rightly, we see ourselves rightly. When we know how holy and glorious He is, and by comparison how unholy we are, we understand our great need for Him. And when we see through the lens of the gospel, that this mighty God gives us His righteousness through Christ as a free gift, how could we be anything but humble? It is only when we forget this astounding truth that we slip into pride.

> **All heresies are a response either to something God said that we don't agree with or to something God commanded that we don't want to obey.**

Humility comes as a matter of course when we keep God's greatness and goodness within our constant sight.

In this place of total dependance on God, we will say as Isaiah did, "Here I am! Send me" (v. 8b).

A small boat moved quietly down the Nile. The moon was nowhere to be seen, and darkness gave the men cover as they carefully navigated the river. Athanasius thanked God for His protection and sat serenely while the boatmen glanced nervously from bank to bank.

Athanasius had been banished from Alexandria again. Though this had become a regular occurrence, it didn't make the pain any less acute. He was a man of action. He wanted to be in the center of church life, serving, teaching, giving of himself to the people he loved so deeply.

But in the pain, there was peace. He knew God would bring justice.

He felt the boat turn toward the western bank, and he saw the distant light of torches along the shore. Soon, they were moored in a shallow inlet. On the upper bank, staring down at them like sentinels against the night sky, were twelve frail men in rough tunics. They stood silently as Athanasius made his way up the foot trail.

At the center of the group was an old man wrapped in an animal-skin coat. Athanasius couldn't believe the man had made the journey on foot to meet him here. Why hadn't he just sent the younger ones to welcome him? But before he could protest, the elderly man stepped toward him, and with the dexterity of someone much younger, knelt and began to kiss the feet of Athanasius. His aged and brittle voice broke the silence. "How beautiful on the mountains are the feet of those who bring the good news."

Athanasius remembered how he had felt in Nicaea, in the room with all those great men who had fought so hard to preserve the true message of the gospel. He felt that same holy love lay heavy on him again. Never at a loss for words, all he could manage to speak was, "Thank you, Father."

They began their walk to the monastery. The elderly monk walking beside him led a great network of holy men living alone in the desert, given to fasting and intercession. During his many times of exile, Athanasius would come under their careful watch and protection. They would move him to countless hiding places as the imperial army hunted him throughout all of Egypt.

After walking in silence for some time, Athanasius was no longer able to hold it in. "Father," he blurted, "I want to go back to Alexandria and resist them openly!" His words sounded crude in the company of such quiet men.

The monk stopped walking. With a smile on his face, he stared into the night sky. "When I was a younger man," he said, "I remember being overcome by the great suffering of our world. Tyrants and kings having their way while the poor and helpless were left defenseless against their violence. I was angry."

He paused, reliving the memory. "I saw the snares the enemy lays out for us. I cried to God, 'What can get through such snares?'" The old man turned to look at Athanasius, and his voice trembled with holy fire. "I heard a voice say to me, 'Humility.' My son, don't forget that you are not fighting men—you are fighting the spirits that afflict them. And you are not the one with the power to defeat them. Submit your heart to God, and He alone will cause your enemies to scatter."

They continued walking in silence under the light of the torches as they approached one of the many desert hiding places in which Athanasius would lie unseen for the next six years.

Some of the worst acts in history were right things done in the wrong way. Being on the side of truth carries its own danger. Chiefly, that of pride.

We are currently in the midst of our own culture wars and there are very real lies and harmful ideas being perpetuated in our time. We must certainly speak up against these things in our appropriate spheres of influence. But how do we do that?

I think the most important question we should ask ourselves when we are being drawn into a debate about something is, "Do I truly have God's love for this person?" If you can't honestly say yes, then wait until you can.

I believe we are ready to have difficult conversations with others only when we have first gone to God in prayer and asked for His compassion on those we are engaging. If we don't love them, then why are we even "fighting for the truth" in the first place? Because ultimately, the reason God cares about truth is because He cares about people. And if we lose that care for others, then we ourselves have fallen into deception.

The pride that can come from being right can be just as harmful as the damage that wrong ideas bring. We must stand for truth, yes, but the way in which we stand must be drenched in the love of God.

Athanasius's life is an instructive model for us today. I don't believe we are called to go around picking fights about ideas, but when we are on the side of the truth, the fight will often find us. There is a difference between fighting *for* truth and fighting *against* people. We are called to love people while at the same time resisting the lies that damage those people.

Where can we find boldness to stand for the truth? We find it, once again, in true humility. Humility, total dependance on God, not only protects our own hearts from heresies but will also give us courage to fight them.

When we live in complete dependence on God, we do not need the approval of rulers, influencers, or peers, because we have the approval of the one true God. However, if we do *not* have this assurance of complete reliance on Him, we will crumble under the weight and pressure to conform to new heresies.

Humility is the secret key for courage. When we are inwardly submitted to God, we will be outwardly courageous in the world. A yielded heart of flesh will give us a backbone of steel.

The great believers of old were able to withstand persecution not because they were strong, but because they knew they were weak, and they relied solely on God's strength.

Final Brushstrokes

In the story of Athanasius and the Arian controversy, we see that God is a God of truth. He *is* the truth. Our portrait of God doesn't have to be muddied and confused by wrong ideas. There can be clear lines and defined features to His face. There will always be mystery, of course, because God is limitless and so far above our knowledge. But just because His depths are unsearchable doesn't mean His character is unknowable. He proved this to us by coming close as the Son of God, fully man and fully divine.

Athanasius gave his entire life for this one effort: to give the world an accurate picture of Jesus, one that showed that He was truly and fully God. And if we live with love and humility, we, too, can stand for the truth in our age, showing the world what God is really like.

Discussion Questions

1. Objective truth really does exist. But our culture thinks otherwise and says that you can make your own truth. Why is it important for us to hold fast to that which is true and lovingly resist that which is false?

2. Arianism was a heresy that didn't see Jesus as fully God. What heresies do you see in our own age?

3. Humility means having total dependence on God. Heresies come from not submitting to God. The antidote to heresy is humility. How can we foster that dependence on God and trusting obedience to His Word?

4. Athanasius was willing to endure extreme suffering in order to stand for the truth. What would produce that kind of fortitude in someone? And how can we model that in our time?

Chapter 9

"THE REAL YOU"— HOW GOD'S IDENTITY FORMS OURS

It was New Year's Day, and I was struggling. I had way too many res-olutions written down in my journal—I was already overwhelmed, and it was only lunchtime. I turned to a blank page. I took a deep breath and remembered that all the things I wanted to change in my life were going to come from a power that was not mine. That my real identity wasn't in a collection of desired habits but was actually hidden in another person, Jesus Christ. So I began to write this to myself as a personal encouragement and reminder:

> The real you is in Jesus.
> It's not in a plan.
> It's not in a person.
> It's not in a movement.
> It's not in a job.
> It's not in a body.
> It's not in a brand.
> It's not in a following.
> The real you is in Jesus.
> It's not in a feeling.
> It's not in a failure.
> It's not in a future.
> It's not in a past.
> The real you is in Jesus.
> The real you is love.
> The real you is joy.
> The real you is peace.
> The real you is life.
> The real you is in Jesus.

Run to Him, He'll show you.

Talk to Him, He'll tell you.

Rest with Him, He'll heal you.

Walk with Him, He'll lead you.

Lean on Him, He'll hold you.

Follow Him, He'll surprise you.

Dream with Him, He'll amaze you.

Cry out to Him, He'll rescue you.

Believe on Him, He'll save you.

The real you is in Jesus.

Ingredients of Identity Crisis

Our culture is in a great identity crisis. How did we get here? As humans, we have always looked for meaning and purpose. Ancient cultures found that meaning in the common goals of the tribe. Most of their time was spent working on very practical things for the survival of their community: farming, building, fighting, hunting, child-rearing. They had to focus on immediate needs, so they didn't have the time or the choice to ask the questions: "What do I want to be?" or "What could I spend my time doing today?"

In modern Western cultures, most of us live in prosperity and stability. Hunger pangs don't drive our day or define our purpose. Most of us aren't worried about where the next meal will come from. Sure, we all need jobs to pay our bills. But many of those bills come from unnecessary things like entertainment, hobbies, junk food, travel, and luxurious overuse of utilities like electricity, water, and gas. Often, our financial stress is self-imposed.

We find ourselves in a world of relative ease and freedom. This allows us to give an unprecedented amount of energy and attention to ourselves. We roll our eyes when we hear that this generation is self-obsessed, and we get tired of hearing thatl label. But maybe the reason this term is used is because it's actually true. And could it be that we're a little defensive because the truth hurts?

Free Morals

During the sixties, the now infamous "sexual revolution" commenced. It wasn't just sexual prohibitions that experienced a revolution—there was also an overall resistance against what was seen as suffocating moralism of traditional institutions. Many of these young people had grown up in postwar "Mayberry" America. They were raised by men who had been to war and bore the mental and physical scars. They were raised by women who for the most part had been silenced in the culture.

The government had been lying to the public about Vietnam over the course of three presidential administrations, and the body count kept getting higher. The church had made its mistakes and was seen by this new generation as cold and legalistic. The scourge of racism still had a strong hold on the nation. And postwar materialism was reaching its frenzied fever pitch.

What was really needed was a moral revolution, a return to the purity of truth and goodness. Instead, there was moral demolition. A mistrust in institutions exploded into outright hatred of traditional moral norms. The crowning achievement of this moral "liberation" was *Roe v. Wade*.

In reality, there were godly corrections available for all these problems. The Bible speaks against materialism, corrupt government, sexism, racism, and cold and hateful religion. Our enemy has his "solutions" for these problems too, but they always end in death and decay. God's solutions are deep, holistic, and life-bringing.

The End Result

What do you get when you have steady moral decay for decades, accompanied by a financial freedom that only perpetuates it? You get something that looks like our modern cultural climate.

We're a generation that has been given the greatest technological powers in human history ... just at the time of our lowest moral fortitude, and we see the destructive results.

This brings us to our identity crisis. The Bible tells us who we are, but what happens when we hate and ridicule the very book that can hold our society together? When we reject God's way of living and intoxicate ourselves with the power of our technological advances?

I love how Paul drills this home in the opening of Ephesians.

- "even as He chose us in him before the foundation of the world." (1:4)

- "He predestined us for adoption to Himself." (1:5)

- "having been predestined according to the purpose of Him who works all things according to the counsel of His will." (1:11)

- "having the eyes of your hearts enlightened, that you may know what is the hope to which He has called you." 1:18)

- "For we are his workmanship, created in Christ Jesus for good works, which God prepared beforehand, that we should walk in them." (2:10)

A Very Big Lie

When it comes to talking about our personal identity, we can't escape a massive lie we hear daily. The lie of "I am what I feel."

Let me give you an example. As I am writing this, I am physically tired. I feel a bit foggy, and my shoulders feel tense from a long day of work, parenting, traffic, and consuming far too much sugar and coffee. Now I have a choice to make. One option before me is to say, "I don't *feel* like writing." And that would be true, because right now I don't feel like doing anything but sleeping. But ... this amazing thing is happening. My fingers are moving on the keyboard. My mind is connecting thoughts. Although I *feel* physically drained, I can still write!

So often, we stop at our feelings. We don't feel like praying, so we don't pray. We don't feel like going to church, so we don't go. The reason we do this is because we've believed a lie. We live in a culture that caters to our feelings (and makes a lot of money doing it). Because we live in the most prosperous time in human history and we're inundated with advertising that tells us we deserve to indulge and to chase our dreams, our hearts begin to be shaped by this new paradigm.

I must confess, the reason I am so passionate about killing this lie is that I have fallen for it over and over again. I still find myself so lost in my feelings that I have to stop and step back from them. I have to imagine I can float above my life and look at it. I have to get above the noise of my feelings to see the truth of what my life actually looks like.

Which brings me to my next point: How do we get out of the gutter of our feelings and on to the clean and healthy path of truth?

Gratitude

Now it's your turn to get a better view of your life. Let's say you're sitting at your kitchen table right now. Imagine yourself levitating about five feet upward and looking out onto your life.

If I were doing this, I would see my beautiful wife at the piano or buzzing around the house getting something done. I would see my four-year-old in a Spider-Man costume trying to do backflips off the couch. I would see my seven-year-old trying to catch the four-year-old Spider-Man mid-backflip. I would see my thirteen-year-old on the edge of the couch with his face in a book bigger than his head. I would see my ten-year-old girl in her happy place practicing for a TV baking competition. And I would see my six-month-old baby boy in his rocking crib playing with his pacifier.

No matter how bad I might have been feeling when I sat down at the table (tired, depressed, frustrated), I can guarantee you it would melt away the instant I "floated" above my family.

Oftentimes, we think that gratitude involves groveling before the feet of God and rattling off a thousand things we're thankful for when actually it's just taking our eyes off of ourselves and putting them on the things God has given us. Gratitude starts with seeing. You can't be thankful for something you're ignoring.

G. K. Chesterton wrote some great passages on this in *Orthodoxy*. He described how his first impressions of the divine came from simply being amazed by the world around him. That the fairy tales he read as a child taught him a way to see the "magic" that infused the world. In his words: "In short, I had always believed that the world involved magic: now I thought that perhaps it involved a magician."[1] One of the surest ways to a practical atheism is to stop noticing the world God has made ... and the God who made it. Chesterton put it this way:

> Children are grateful when Santa Claus puts in their stockings gifts of toys or sweets. Could I not be grateful to Santa Claus when he put in my stockings the gift of two miraculous legs? We thank people for birthday presents of cigars and slippers. Can I thank no one for the birthday present of birth?[2]

We take for granted the startling fact that we are alive. That our loved ones are alive. That God in His loving-kindness has granted us the privilege of existing.

The way to get out of the prison of our feelings and into the wide world of grace is to first *notice* the startling and beautiful world that surrounds us. Then we will sense the startling and beautiful God who created it and has a purpose for our lives. We will remember that we are not the sum total of our emotions but the sum total of His design!

And no matter what we may feel at the moment (which has more to do with how we slept or what we've eaten than with our true nature), we will remember that a very good and loving God has placed this life before us. He has placed us right in the middle of this moment. All we have to do is look up and appreciate what He has given, and then He gives us the grace to go and steward it well.

Vulnerable

Your body and soul are vulnerable because they are exposed to the elements of this world. That's why the Bible says to guard your heart (see Prov. 4:23) and put on the armor of God to protect yourself from the schemes of the enemy (see Eph. 6:10–17).

But if your body and soul are vulnerable to the world and the enemy, how much more vulnerable are they to God? God has given believers the capacity to choose whom to plug into. Whom do we orient ourselves toward?

> Gratitude starts with seeing.
> You can't be thankful for
> something you're ignoring.

When we turn ourselves toward God and choose to be influenced by Him, our body and soul do not resist His goodness.

Your body and your soul aren't bad—they're just "in process." They have been fully redeemed by God, but they remain in the process of being transformed by God. Your body and your soul belong to God and are saved: "bought with a price" (see 1 Cor. 6:19–20). It's just that they are still on a battleground and the bullets are flying!

In battle, you can get injured from an attack or by a mistake you make. A soldier is at least as likely to take a wrong step and hurt himself by falling as he is of getting shot. And until Jesus comes back, your body and soul are continually being renewed by your act of choosing God daily.

That's what the apostle Paul meant by dying daily (see 1 Cor. 15:31). His body didn't feel like getting up and traveling all those miles to preach the gospel. His soul got discouraged when those closest to him let him down. Yet he didn't live according to those things. He lived according to the Spirit. And as a result, his body and soul began to line up with who he really was: a great man of God.

You are amazing! So often we make final judgments on ourselves because of a mistake we made on the battlefield. Get up! The Father has forgiven you. Walk according to your true nature! You are the righteousness of God in Christ (see 2 Cor. 5:21)! The real you is in Jesus.

You Don't Have to Be an Influencer

The one thing I can't help but notice when I read the story of Jesus' birth is that there could have been more fanfare. It goes against everything we've been trained to value in our modern culture.

Here we have *God* being born as a baby to save the *world*, and there are no power brokers there. No kings or dignitaries. Just some animals. His parents. So ordinary.

And while we live on our digital stages with bulbs flashing and shutters clicking, streaming our lives to the ends of the earth, we look upon this nativity and see God born in silent obscurity.

There was an announcement, though! God did send out a heavenly press release.

To shepherds.

In the back country.

"Peace on earth! Good will to men!"

The most monumental piece of information since the Ten Commandments ... entrusted to men who smelled of sheep.

Influencers. We love influencers. We are so worried that our messages won't be heard and our stories won't be seen, and yet God goes to the guys with no "influence." This story tells us that God doesn't need influencers. He didn't need the Sanhedrin or the Roman power players to know. He wanted the humble to hear. Because the humble one was coming to save the humble ... and to use the humble.

Jesus, the consummate "insider," the One who knows *everything*, privy to all the grand decisions made from the throne, comes to hang out with the people on the edges of society!

Jesus didn't need influencers because He *was* the influencer. He would influence twelve so deeply as to turn their lives inside out. And those disciples would turn the world upside down.

He didn't need fanfare because His success never depended on fanfare. His success depended on humility, which is utter dependance on the Father.

This we see in His birth.

Do you feel like you're on the outside of the important meetings? Not in the "in" crowd? Take heart because God loves you and values you. He sees you as an integral part of His redemptive plan.

When Jesus transforms us, we stop seeing the popular and the powerful as people to be envied or hated. They are people to be loved. People He can use! But He doesn't need their influence—they need His. *We* need His. Our real identity is in Him because He is everything. And now it is our privilege to search out the treasures of His goodness in relationship with Him.

Discussion Questions

1. "The real you is in Jesus." If you are a follower of Christ, your true identity is in Him. The more you become like Him, the more you'll become like your true self, the one He destined you to be. In what way is the world pulling you away from this truth? How would your life be different if you lived out of this new identity that you have in Christ?

2. Our culture has believed the lie that "you are what you feel." In what ways have your feelings misled you and kept you from being all that God has made you to be?

3. Gratitude starts with seeing, which means you can't be grateful for something you're ignoring. What are some good things in your life that you've had the tendency to overlook? Things that, if you were grateful for, would change your whole perspective on life?

Chapter 10

"THE TREASURE"—
THE REASON
WE EXIST

The most startling reality in the universe is that God wants to have an intimate relationship with us.

If you've grown up in the church, you may be numb to it. If you're a nonbeliever, you may be unsure about it. And if you have a burning heart for God, you are overjoyed by it. But whatever your response, the shocking fact remains that God wants to know us and wants to be known by us.

In His Sermon on the Mount (see Matt. 5–7), Jesus gives us a behind-the-scenes glimpse into the priorities of heaven:

> Not everyone who says to me, "Lord, Lord," will enter the kingdom of heaven, but the one who does the will of my Father who is in heaven. On that day many will say to me, "Lord, Lord, did we not prophesy in your name, and cast out demons in your name, and do many mighty works in your name?" And then will I declare to them, "I never knew you; depart from me, you workers of lawlessness." (Matt. 7:21–23)

"I never knew you."

Here, God lets us in on His deepest desire for us. He wants to know us, and He wants us to know Him.

But doesn't God already know *everyone* since He created us?

The Greek word that is translated as "knew" in this verse is versatile and doesn't just mean a general knowledge. It can also mean an intimate relationship. The same Greek word was used in Matthew 1:25 when it speaks about Joseph and Mary not having sex: "[He] knew her not until she had given birth to a son."

So when the all-knowing God says, "I never knew you," He cannot be talking about a general knowledge (because He knows everything). He is talking about an intimate, experiential knowing that can come only through relationship.

I heard someone once say, "Salvation isn't the plan of God. Salvation is what gets us back to the plan of God." I like that. Salvation was a sub-plan to get us back to the primary plan. And that plan was for us to have a thriving relationship with the living God.

God's highest desire for you isn't that you just pray a prayer and believe in Jesus. His highest desire is for you to know Him. And this is possible only through trusting in Jesus' work of salvation.

God's goal is to get you back in right relationship with Himself. And that is the treasure Jesus died to give us: the mind-blowing privilege of knowing God.

I have been through some dark times in my life. I've struggled with depression and mental health challenges. But the one thing that has gotten me through all of it has been knowing God.

To have the assurance that He is there with me, no matter what I do, no matter how much I've failed Him—this truth has literally saved my life.

We were designed to be in communion with Him. We are at our worst when we are running from this reality. Hiding from God is like hiding from oxygen: it just doesn't make sense for us. Not only does it go against our flourishing, but hiding from Him goes against our very survival.

The greatest gift is that we get to know Him deeply. This is a forever journey. And the one, unchanging constant is Him. He will never leave us, because of the work Jesus did, and we always get access to *Him*, no matter what we go through. He can be your point of reference in an increasingly confusing and upside-down world.

The people we have talked about in this book did not just know about God—they actually found Him. And when they found Him, they understood that He really is enough.

I want to end this book with a few practical steps to knowing God.

How do you come to the place with God that C. S. Lewis, Augustine, the Booths, Athanasius, Thomas Chalmers, and Fanny Crosby were? Well, there is no cookie-cutter solution, and everyone is different, but we can know God just as they did.

Here are four steps we can take now to grow closer to God and unlock the treasure of knowing Him deeply.

Be with Him

Our first and greatest privilege is to simply *be* with God. To just sit with Him and enjoy His nearness is the gift Jesus died to give us.

We have been so affected by the industrial revolution and free-market economics that we think everything in life has to have productive output. Including us as followers of the Lord. We have to lay this idea down when we come near to God. This is God we're talking about! He doesn't need our feverish efforts or absurd spiritual performances. He loves us and wants to be with us. And we *need* to be with Him.

So, the first step you can take to knowing God more is to just sit with Him.

Now this is going to get awkward really quickly because we don't know how to sit. Silence and stillness are learned skills, but they are essential if we are to grow in God.

Start with two minutes. Get in a quiet place, close your eyes, and just think about God. Your mind will wander, and that's okay. When it does, don't chide yourself. Gently bring your attention back to Him. The more you do this, the more it will transform from a duty into a delight, because you will be doing the most important thing a human can do: giving your attention to God.

> Our first and greatest privilege is to simply *be* with God. To just sit with Him and enjoy His nearness is the gift Jesus died to give us.

During your two minutes, you might meditate on one of the attributes we've discussed in this book: God's love, joy, compassion, holiness, power, and so on. You can also ponder a scripture while using your imagination to focus on God. If you draw near to Him like this, it is inevitable that you will begin to feel His presence.

Talk to Him

The second thing you can do is simply talk to God.

You can use the ACTS model of prayer, if you like:

A—Adoration

C—Confession

T—Thanksgiving

S—Supplication[1]

Adoration is lifting your heart to Him in worship and praise. Just open your mouth and speak or sing of His greatness and goodness. The Psalms are wonderful for language to get you started. Psalm 146 is a good one. As you make a practice of opening your mouth and worshipping Him, your life will be changed. When Jesus gave us a model for prayer, He began with, "Our Father in heaven, hallowed be your name" (Matt. 6:9). Praising and honoring God is fundamental to our interactions with Him. It is the birthplace of prayer.

Then, *confession*. Be honest with him. Are you struggling with fear? Tell Him. Are you dealing with shame? Tell Him! Just be open with God. He already knows anyway, so why would you try to hide your heart from Him? Tell Him every sin you've committed that comes to mind that you haven't yet asked forgiveness for, and repent. Repentance is turning away from that sin. It is asking Him for grace to break free from whatever habit or hang-up it is. As you talk to God, be raw and open. This brings healing! (See James 5:16.)

After all, what is a relationship if you are never truthful about what is going on in your heart? Honesty is the key to intimacy.

First John 1:9 says, "If we confess our sins, he is faithful and just to forgive us our sins and to cleanse us from all unrighteousness." And 1 Peter 5:7 tells us to cast our cares on Him because He cares for us.

Next is *thanksgiving*. The practice of gratitude is noticing every good thing in your life, naming those things, and acknowledging God as their source. Thanksgiving is a wonderful way to talk to God. And it will radically change the way you see your life.

Finally, there is *supplication.* That's a fancy word for bringing your needs and desires to God. Do you have a loved one who is struggling? Pray that he or she would be healed or encouraged. Are you struggling with fear or doubt? Ask God for peace and faith!

> Ask, and it will be given to you; seek, and you will find; knock, and it will be opened to you. For everyone who asks receives, and the one who seeks finds, and to the one who knocks it will be opened. (Matt. 7:7–8)

The ACTS progression is a simple model to get you going. The main thing is that you regularly talk to God. Praying every day throughout the day will change your life, and you will begin to know God on a deeper level.

Listen to Him

Another thing we can do to know God more is to listen to Him. How do we do that? The first way is to read His Word. The Bible is God's voice speaking to us. He moved within men over the course of thousands of years to give us this book. If you want to know what His voice sounds like, begin to drench your mind in the Scriptures. The book of John is a great place to start.

A good resource for this is Dr. George Grant's Keystone notebooks. It is based on a Bible study tool that Thomas Chalmers developed and will help you fill you heart with God's Word.

The more you read the Bible, the more you recognize God's voice. The Holy Spirit will begin to speak to you and guide you, though never in any way that contradicts the Bible. A great resource on learning to hear God's voice is a book called *Whisper* by Mark Batterson.

Begin listening because He wants to speak to you—through His Word and through the active voice of the Holy Spirit.

Obey Him

Finally, a great accelerator in knowing God is simply obeying what He tells us to do. Not from a place of trying to impress Him or earn anything, but just because of His love and goodness.

> As the Father has loved me, so have I loved you. Abide in my love. If you keep my commandments, you will abide in my love, just as I have kept my Father's commandments and abide in his love. These things I have spoken to you, that my joy may be in you, and that your joy may be full. (John 15:9–11)

Here, Jesus is inviting us into what I call a cycle of joy.

First, we abide in His love. This is what I was focusing on when I talked about being with and adoring God. When we enjoy His love, it empowers us to obey His commands.

But then something amazing happens: when we obey His commands, we experience more of His love! Abiding in God's love gives us power to obey. And obeying God gives us more of His love.

God wants us to get "stuck" in this cycle of joy! Jesus wants your joy to be full.

Obeying God is actually an opportunity to encounter more of His goodness. His goodness will lead to more obedience. And, by God's grace, the cycle will continue as long as you keep responding to Him.

It's All about Him

Being with God, talking to God, listening to God, and obeying God is not about what we are doing. It is about experiencing who He is.

Remember, the gospel is not "do and live"; it is "believe and live." The reason we seek after God is to get Him. All life, joy, and peace flow from His nature.

The people whose stories I have just shared can attest that God is better than we think He is. And it is our mission to go and tell the world about His goodness. To use our gifts to "paint God" for a world that is desperate to know what He is really like.

Discussion Questions

1. "The most startling reality in the universe is that God wants to have an intimate relationship with us." Why is it amazing that God would want to have a relationship with us? And how can we better steward this privilege?

2. We have been so affected about the productivity standards of our time that it's often hard for us to just sit and simply be with God. Have you tried the exercise of sitting in silence and focusing your thoughts and affections on God? What was that experience like?

3. A helpful guide for prayer is the ACTS model (adoration, confession, thanksgiving, and supplication). Which one of these are you most comfortable with? Which ones are you least comfortable with?

CONCLUSION

Knowing God changes us. As the stories in this book reveal, when we come to know the character of God, it will always have a transformative effect on our character.

Unfortunately, all wrong ideas about God also have a profound impact on how we live. The key to behavioral change is to get the right picture of God. When our portrait of Him is confused, blurred, and damaged by untruth, we ourselves will be damaged as well. But as we restore our vision of Him, healing begins.

In the life of C. S. Lewis, we see a young man who was broken and hurting from the loss of his mother as a child and the brutality of the First World War. But his atheism was demolished by the most unlikely thing of all: the joy of God. He found that the very God he could not believe in was actually the source of everything he had ever loved.

Saint Augustine of Hippo desperately sought fulfillment through the lusts of the body and the striving of the mind. His image of God had been marred by the lie that all his pleasures and knowledge would be stripped from him if he ever gave in to God. But to his surprise, he found that this holy God who demanded everything actually wanted to give him everything. That the personal holiness God requires is not a taking, but a giving. That when God requires our obedience, He secures our freedom.

When our portrait of Him is confused, blurred, and damaged by untruth, we ourselves will be damaged as well. But as we restore our vision of Him, healing begins.

In the story of Kathryn Kuhlman, we see someone who was willing to take the risk to believe that God's miracle power is still at work today. Her picture of God was not one frozen in an inactive distance. She knew a God who comes close and heals the sick today just as He did two thousand years ago.

Her story invites us into a topic that for many of us carries a lot of pain and questions. Many mysteries surround the subject of miraculous healing. But we see that God is with us amid our questions, and no matter the outcome when we pray for the sick, we know God is still good and wise. We learn that taking the risk to believe for someone's healing is an act of love regardless of the results.

The lives of William and Catherine Booth paint the portrait of God as one whose compassion carries great energy, driving us to the hardest places to care for those in need. They show that God's love was not just an intellectual concept to be considered but a clarion call urging us on to serve the hurting. When we live this way, the world will see an accurate image of God—the image Jesus depicted of the father who ran to the lost son and showered him with extravagant and undeserved affection. William and Catherine Booth show us that we are capable of truly monumental things when we grasp God's compassion for us and the world.

Fanny Crosby shows us an image of a God who is faithful and present even in deep suffering. In her story, we see that we can know His faithfulness not in spite of our suffering but because of it. Fanny's blindness enabled her to hear the songs of heaven with unusual clarity. Her prolific output of gospel hymns testified to people all over the world about the faithfulness and goodness of God.

Finally, in the story of Athanasius, we see a God who cares deeply about the truth. He cannot lie, and our lives must be given to defending that truth. Athanasius paid a great price to remain faithful to the gospel in a culture that was swiftly giving in to attractive heresies. We see that God's love and truth cannot be separated, so we must fight for truth without compromising the way of love. We can simply say what is right, all the while carrying the depths of God's love and compassion for those who are being led astray.

Our souls need a beautiful and accurate painting of God's character. If we can see Him as He is, in His love, power, holiness, joy, and truth, we will be conformed into that very nature. The world is desperate for a true glimpse of Him, and with His help, we can live lives that show them what He is really like.

NOTES

Chapter 1

1. C. S. Lewis, *Mere Christianity* (New York: Macmillan, 1953), 136.

Chapter 2

1. C. S. Lewis, *Surprised by Joy* (New York: Harcourt Brace Jovanovich, 1955), 72.

2. Lewis, *Surprised by Joy*, 78.

3. Lewis, *Surprised by Joy*, 168.

4. Lewis, *Surprised by Joy*, 238.

5. Lewis, *Surprised by Joy*, 228–29.

6. G. K. Chesterton, *Orthodoxy* (New York: Image, Doubleday, 2001), 170.

Chapter 3

1. "שָׁדַק" Blue Letter Bible Lexicon, accessed December 7, 2023, www.blueletterbible.org/lexicon/h6944/kjv/wlc/0-1/.

2. Graham Cooke, "Wild Love 2018–Graham Cooke," Charlotte, NC, recorded August 23–25, 2018, YouTube video, 23:49, www.youtube.com/watch?v=oNi_s7129Os.

3. Todd White, "Todd White–Remaining Humble & Keeping Your Heart Right," posted April 29, 2017, YouTube video, 50:06, www.youtube.com/watch?v=-Risr31QFyo.

4. Dietrich Bonhoeffer, *Discipleship*, Dietrich Bonhoeffer Works, vol. 4 (Minneapolis : Fortress, 2003), Kindle, chap. 1.

5. James Strong, *The Exhaustive Concordance of the Bible* (Nashville: Abingdon, 1890), Kindle edition, G4053.

Chapter 4

1. Mark Cahill, *One Thing You Can't Do in Heaven* (Stone Mountain, GA: Mark Cahill, 2002).

2. Reinhard Bonnke, *Hell Empty, Heaven Full* (New Kensington, PA: Whitaker House, 2006), Kindle edition, chap.13.

3. "A Global Movement," The Salvation Army International Development Australia, accessed December 7, 2023, www.salvationarmy.org.au/international-development/about /the-salvation-army-a-global-movement/.

4. Lindsay Deutsch and Veronica Bravo, "On 150th Anniversary, Stats on Salvation Army's Impact," *USA Today*, July 2, 2015, www.usatoday.com/story/news/nation-now/2015/07/02 /salvation-army-150th-anniversary/29596003/.

Chapter 5

1. Kathryn Kuhlman, "It Cost You Everything," Facebook, posted by Holy Spirit TV, July 28, 2021, www.facebook.com/watch /?v=3926608974132693.

2. "40 More Bill Johnson Quotes," Prayer Coach, accessed October 18, 2023, https://prayer-coach.com/bill-johnson-quotes/.

Chapter 6

1. Timothy Keller, "Tim Keller on How to Bring the Gospel to Post-Christian America," posted by Carey Nieuwhof, May 11, 2020, YouTube, 00:13:30, www.youtube.com/watch?v=zNve 3Hexh28&t=821s.

2. William Wilberforce, *A Practical View of the Prevailing Religious System of Professed Christians, in the Middle and Higher Classes in This Country, Contrasted with Real Christianity* (London: T. Caddell, 1797).

Chapter 7

1. Isaac Watts, "Alas! And Did My Savior Bleed" (1707), Public Domain.

2. J Lind, "Letter to the Editor," *For What It's Worth* (2019), copyright J Lind.

Chapter 8

1. "Homoousios," Theopedia, accessed April 16, 2024, https://www.theopedia.com/homoousios.

2. "The Nicene Creed," Reformed Church in America, accessed December 7, 2023, www.rca.org/about/theology/creeds-and -confessions/the-nicene-creed/.

3. Andrew Murray, *Humility* (London: James Nisbet & Co., 1896), 12.

Chapter 9

1. G. K. Chesterton, *Orthodoxy* (New York: Image, Doubleday, 2001), 59.

2. Chesterton, *Orthodoxy*, 52.

Chapter 10

1. R. C. Sproul, "A Simple Acrostic for Prayer," Ligonier, June 25, 2018, www.ligonier.org/learn/articles/simple-acrostic-prayer.

FURTHER
READING

Kuhlman, Kathryn. *I Believe in Miracles*, Pyramid Publications, 1969.

McGrath, Alister. *C. S. Lewis - A Life: Eccentric Genius, Reluctant Prophet*, Tyndale Elevate, 2013.

Lewis, *C. S. Surprised by Joy: The Shape of My Early Life*, Harper One, 2017.

Finlayson, Sandy. *Chief Scottish Man: The Life and Ministry of Thomas Chalmers,* Evangelical Press, 2021.

Chalmers, Thomas. *The Expulsive Power of a New Affection*, Crossway, 2020.

Benge, Janey and Geoff. *William Booth: Soup, Soap, & Salvation*, YWAM Publishing, 2012.

Tyson, John R. *The Great Athanasius: An Introduction to His Life and Work*, Cascade Books, 2017.

Saint Augustine. *Confessions*, Oxford University Press, 2008.

Crosby, Fanny. *Fanny Crosby: An Autobiography*, Hendrickson Publishers, 2015.